THE WILDERNESS GUIDE TO
DUTCH OVEN COOKING

THE WILDERNESS GUIDE TO
DUTCH OVEN COOKING

INCREDIBLE RECIPES FOR YOUR NEXT OUTDOOR ADVENTURE

KATE ROWINSKI,

AUTHOR OF *THE PRESSURE COOKER COOKBOOK*

PHOTOGRAPHY BY JIM ROWINSKI

Skyhorse Publishing

Skyhorse Publishing books may be purchased in bulk at special discounts for sales promotion, corporate gifts, fund-raising, or educational purposes. Special editions can also be created to specifications. For details, contact the Special Sales Department, Skyhorse Publishing, 307 West 36th Street, 11th Floor, New York, NY 10018 or info@skyhorsepublishing.com.

Skyhorse® and Skyhorse Publishing® are registered trademarks of Skyhorse Publishing, Inc.®, a Delaware corporation.

www.skyhorsepublishing.com

10 9 8 7 6 5 4 3 2 1

Library of Congress Cataloging-in-Publication Data is available on file.

Paperback ISBN: 978-1-5107-7870-2
eBook ISBN: 978-1-5107-7918-1

Printed in China

Contents

Introduction

I am not sure there was ever a day in my entire childhood when I did not come home to my mom's Dutch oven simmering on the stove or in the oven. She had a collection of ovens, some flat-bottomed, others made for camp with their three squat little legs. Mom's entire cooking repertoire revolved around the Dutch oven, whether we were at camp on the Louisiana bayou, on a fishing trip in northern Wisconsin, or just having a weeknight dinner at home. Mom grew up in Louisiana, in the heart of Cajun country. Louisiana cooks are at their best outdoors; they just seem to have a knack for gathering together good ingredients, good fun, and good people to turn every meal into an event.

When I met my husband, he came with a collection of cast iron, too. He had a number of different skillet sizes that he carried in his Ford camper. He used them for searing trout, cooking up a batch of fried potatoes, or frying up ham and eggs. While the Dutch oven was not part of his culinary repertoire, he certainly had a touch for getting the coals just right for frying up quick meals.

My husband proposed to me after a campfire meal. We had made a long, hard paddle up the Brule River in northern Wisconsin on a late fall day that had more than a hint of snow in the air. It was not a good day for fishing, but Jim was in the mood for an adventure. We cast into the cold air, neither of us believing that a trout would present itself on such a day.

The paddling was difficult against the strong current and I was losing my patience as we struggled to negotiate a particularly difficult passage. As we rounded a bend, Jim hopped out of the canoe and pulled us to shore. We built a fire on a small point jutting out into the river. Jim stripped off his wet pants and socks, wrapping a plaid wool blanket around his waist. As I arranged his wet clothes near the fire, he surprised me by pulling out a picnic luncheon: a giant slice of ham, potatoes for frying, and two large apples. We set the iron skillet on the fire to heat and he pulled out a bottle of wine and two real glass goblets. We shared it laughing, aware that the day and the conditions were much better suited to a warm cup of cider and a little bourbon. But we drank it anyway, and it made the perfect accompaniment to the salty ham, crisp potatoes, and fried apples.

After lunch, he climbed onto a large branch overlooking the river. He said he wanted to look for fish, but he soon asked me to join him. Exasperated and a little too cold for comfort, I reluctantly climbed onto the branch with him, looking down at the water to see what was capturing his attention. But when I reached him, I realized he wasn't looking at the water at all. He was holding out a ring. I will never forget the sight of that impossibly young man, swathed in his makeshift wool plaid kilt, holding out the promise of an adventurous future.

That day was the perfect indicator of what our life would be together. Upstream struggles and cold, fishless days, warm fires, good food, fresh air, and rushing rivers—and a dash of adventure in everything we would do. I can't fry a ham steak or make a fry up of potatoes without thinking of that day. Every image, every memory, is captured in the ingredients of a shared meal. For me, that's what outdoor cooking is all about.

I added my first Dutch oven to our set of cookware, and over the years, we learned to make every sort of meal in every kind of condition. After we graduated from college, we set off in our retrofitted VW bus to explore the country. We cooked roasted chicken on hot, steamy days in the Shenandoah Mountains and made venison chili when we portaged the Boundary Waters Canoe Area. We set up elaborate chicken pot pie picnics next to trout streams and made long, elaborate roast beef dinners after sunset in Yellowstone Park. We had outdoor Christmas celebrations over campfires with steaming lamb stew and celebrated birthdays in the middle of the forest with apple gingerbread birthday cake baking in the Dutch oven.

As our family grew, so did our outdoor kitchen, expanding from three skillets and a Dutch oven to a half-dozen skillets, four Dutch ovens, a cooking table, and an ever-expanding pantry of traveling supplies and utensils. We couldn't wait to get out the door to go camping—our menu plans often overshadowing the plans for fishing or hiking.

When we bought our home in Virginia, we finally had room to set up a proper outdoor cooking area. Today this is where we most often grill, fry turkeys, and build the fires for heating our Dutch ovens. Our fire pit is a great place for the family to gather, whether over a pot of stew or roasted mussels, or just with beers and marshmallows for the kids.

After my mom died, I was fortunate enough to inherit her Dutch ovens. I have a special fondness for one in particular, a flat-bottomed oven that I use for simmering stews or frying chicken at home. It evokes all the goodness of childhood, and I am reminded of every recipe

that ever passed through it. The pan itself bears witness to those days, with a rich patina of hard-earned seasoning that remains as good today as it ever was in my mother's day.

For me, Dutch oven cooking is not about the recipes, although I have many. It is not about the techniques, although I have worked hard to master them. For me, Dutch oven cooking is about cooking in beautiful places, creating meals with wonderful people, and sharing the warmth of the soft, dying embers as they signal the end of the day.

Enjoy.

CHAPTER 1

The Basics of Dutch Oven Cooking

The term "Dutch oven" is used to describe any heavy-duty pot with a tight-fitting lid that is used for long, slow cooking. Dutch ovens are made in many configurations, from elegant enameled ovens used in the kitchen oven to heavy flat-bottom ovens designed for stovetops.

For the purpose of camp cooking, the Dutch oven (often referred to as the camp Dutch oven) is a heavy cast-iron pot with a tight-fitting lid and three small legs. This type of oven is designed specifically for cooking over an open heat source. There are also Dutch ovens designed

for outdoor use made of heavy aluminum. They are easier to transport, but have somewhat different heating properties than cast iron.

Consistent temperature control is the key to successful Dutch oven cooking. There are a set of basic principles that guide all Dutch oven cooking, and while it may take a little practice to get the hang of it, learning to create the right heat at the right time will allow you to use your Dutch oven for almost any kind of recipe.

CHOOSE YOUR OVEN

It is inevitable that if you fall in love with Dutch oven cooking the way that we have, you will eventually own several ovens. But if you are just starting out, it may be hard to decide what size to buy. A standard 10 in. (25.5 cm) oven holds about 4 quarts (3.8 liters) and serves 4 people pretty nicely. I prefer a 12 in. (30.5 cm) oven for most of my general cooking. I like having enough space so that a big chicken and a pile of vegetables get the room they need to roast nicely. Many basic recipes are pretty forgiving—you just have to adjust for the fact that a smaller recipe in a larger oven may cook faster than you expected. The major exception is baking. For the best outcome with baked goods, always use the recommended oven size for your recipe.

The standard Dutch oven height is about 3½ in. (8.9 cm). These are ideal for baking and general use. A deeper Dutch oven is also available. At a height of about 5 in. (12.2 cm), it is perfectly suited for accommodating a large roast or bird.

ASSEMBLE YOUR GEAR

A Dutch oven kitchen requires a small but specific set of tools. We pack these items into our "kitchen box" so we never find ourselves afield without some essential piece of equipment.

Wooden Spoons

Assemble a nice collection of wooden spoons and spatulas for cooking with your Dutch oven. Wood is the ideal material because it won't scratch the surface, doesn't conduct heat, and will not melt under high temperature conditions. Plastic utensils, even the ones that are called heat-resistant, can melt or warp. Metal utensils not only scratch the surface but can get really hot and cause a burn.

Leather Gloves

Dutch oven cooking puts you in direct contact with extremely hot conditions. You will be moving charcoals, lifting pots, and turning lids, so it is a good idea to have high-quality hand protection. Some of the tougher chefs in my family scoff at this, and it is true that most chefs have developed a high tolerance for heat over the long years in the kitchen. But hot cast iron and glowing coals should always be taken seriously. That's why I skip the standard pot holder and go with a good leather work glove. My dad was a welder, so early on I became accustomed to heavy welder's gloves around the campfire. I still don't use anything else.

Charcoal Chimney

A charcoal chimney is an essential tool for Dutch oven cooking. A chimney can get your coals lit and ready to use

within twenty minutes or so. Chimneys work by holding the charcoals in a cylinder and lighting them from below using newspaper. The stack of coals lights from bottom to top and are ready when they are about 40–50 percent ashed over. No lighter fluid needed—just spray your newspaper with a little cooking oil spray before lighting it. The oil burns away first, slowing the burning of the paper. Just make sure you place your chimney on a safe, heat-proof surface.

Long-Handled Tongs

Good long-handled tongs are used for moving charcoal briquettes into place. Simple metal ones are best; don't choose tongs with plastic ends.

Parchment Paper

A pack of parchment liners has moved from my nice-to-have column to my absolutely essential column over the years. If you bake, invest in these.

Lid Lifter

Resist the temptation to use your tongs as your lid lifter. Tongs just aren't strong enough to get a good grasp on a heavy lid and can easily slip out of your grasp. And if there are coals on the lid, you need even more control. A Dutch oven lid lifter allows you to grasp the lid or the oven bail and raise it straight up so you don't disturb or topple the coals.

Lid Rest

A lid rest is more than just a convenience for keeping your lid clean. The fact is, lids get really hot. You can't remove them and put them down on just any surface. If you don't want to buy one, keep a sheet tray nearby or make a version yourself. But have a plan for putting down your lid!

Fireplace Shovel

Most of the movement of coals is done with some precision, which is why we use tongs for coal placement. But a small shovel comes in handy for throwing in some coals to warm a cook hole, shoveling extra coals to a new location, or cleaning up ash.

Whisk Broom

A small whisk broom comes in handy for clearing ashes off your oven lid or cleaning your cooking table after everything has cooled.

Dust Covers

Covers made specifically to store Dutch ovens are great for storing out-of-season ovens and transporting dirty ovens. I like the padded type, because they also help protect items traveling with them.

Over time, you will discover your own list of essentials. My husband enjoys using a tripod over an open fire for soups and stews. An ash bucket is handy for safely disposing of warm ashes. Some people always carry a meat thermometer for checking temperatures. I like matches, but many people prefer to keep a propane lighter in their gear box. You will, of course, also create the basics of your own travel kitchen. We keep two large plastic boxes with firmly fitting lids to carry all our "pantry" ingredients as well as our essential kitchen utensils.

USE CHARCOAL BRIQUETTES

While you can certainly use your Dutch oven over a wood campfire, I have found that charcoal briquettes are much easier to use for controlling and maintaining heat. Good charcoal briquettes are a more consistent size than campfire coals, and they burn longer and more evenly. They are easier to move around too, allowing you to adjust your heat quickly and easily. Keep your charcoal briquettes in a sealable container to keep them from getting damp and absorbing too much moisture.

Dutch oven cooking using coals from a wood fire works in the same way as briquette cooking. Hardwood must be used. Soft woods such as pine and poplar burn away too quickly. A wood fire requires about 45 minutes for coals to reach the proper temperature. Wood coals tend to be inconsistent in size and do not last as long as charcoal briquettes, so you have to tend the fire more carefully.

CREATE A GOOD BASE

It is romantic to think of setting up your Dutch oven in a campfire circle, and we have certainly done that. The problem is that the cool earth tends to draw heat from the coals more quickly than we would like. If you do set up on the cold earth, "preheat" the ground with a shovel of coals before getting started.

For a long time, we carried a large flat stone to use as our cooking base. We also sometimes set up our Dutch ovens on heavy-duty grills. Both methods work, but over time we realized that for the best consistency, we needed

to invest in a camp cooking table. These tables allow you to set up your cooking area at cook stove height so you don't have to constantly stoop over a hot fire. They have built-in windscreens that keep your coals sheltered from breezes and reflect heat back to the oven.

FIND A SAFE LOCATION

Set up your cooking area in a location with good ventilation. Never cook inside a tent or in an enclosed area.

Charcoal produces toxic, odorless fumes. Avoid overhanging branches and roofs that could catch fire, as well as wood floor surfaces that might be damaged by falling coals.

Uneven surfaces not only lead to uneven cooking, but with all that hot coal and simmering food, they can be dangerous. If you are cooking on the ground, find a nice flat surface or use a shovel to create one. If you are using a camp cooking table, take a few minutes to select a suitable location. Most cooking tables come with adjustable legs that allow you to quickly create a level base for your Dutch ovens.

SHELTER YOUR FIRE

Even a small breeze can play havoc with your cooking temperatures. If you don't have a cooking table, carry some kind of stove shield in your gear to keep out the wind. Any kind of makeshift breeze block will help you keep your fire burning nicely and prevent ashes from blowing into your food when you lift the lid.

LAY OUT YOUR COALS EVENLY

I like to lay my coals out in a circular pattern, starting about ½ in. inward from the outside of the oven. The key is to create even heat and avoid hot spots that could burn or overcook part of your food.

PREHEAT

I don't think it ever hurts to start with a warm oven, but it is particularly important for some recipes. If your recipe would logically be placed into a preheated oven at home, it is natural that you would start it in your Dutch oven in the same way. Make sure to heat both the oven and the lid. For baked goods, a warm lid is particularly important to get the baking process off to a good start.

BECOME A "POT WATCHER"

You will need to check your heat source pretty often and adjust as needed. Most Dutch oven failures occur because no one is "watching the pot." Part of the fun of cooking in a Dutch oven is watching and adjusting as your food cooks.

Over time, you will get a feel for when you need a little more or less heat here or there. With a good set of long-handled tongs, briquettes can be added, shifted, or removed as needed.

PEEK! (BUT NOT TOO OFTEN)

One of the beautiful things about Dutch oven cooking is that it keeps all that heat and moisture circulating around your food. Because of that, recipes that are designed specifically for the Dutch oven often call for less liquid than standard recipes. In addition, heat that is too high or too low may alter your liquid levels. To get your final product perfectly done, with just the right amount of liquid, check your liquid levels and adjust as necessary.

At first, you will be tempted to peek often. While that is the surest way to see what is happening, resist the temptation and keep the peeking down to every 15 minutes or so. Every time you remove the lid, a bit of your heat and moisture are lost.

GIVE IT A SPIN

Giving your Dutch oven a small turn now and then is a good way to ensure even heat. Simply lift the entire pot and give it a quarter turn and lower it back down to

its heat source. Likewise, lift the lid and turn it a quarter turn to control the top heat. Use a gloved hand and a heavy-duty lid lifter to safely and comfortably lift straight up and place the heavy oven and lid back down without spilling your coals or toppling your food.

STAY ON TOP OF YOUR FUEL SUPPLY

Depending on air temperatures, wind, and humidity conditions, a batch of coals should last for 30–45 minutes. That means that for a recipe calling for an hour or more of cook time, you will need to have a batch of coals on the

side waiting to replace the old ones. Keep your charcoal chimney nearby for starting an extra batch of fuel. When the coals are 80 percent white ash, fill in with a few new coals.

LEARN TO STACK

A multicourse meal does not require a lot of surface space. When you want to cook several things at once, think UP, not OUT. You can use the top coals of one oven as the bottom coals of the next oven. Put your roast on the bottom, add a side dish above. Your entire meal is ready all at once.

FLIP YOUR LID

The lid of the Dutch oven is made from the same heavy-duty heat-proof cast iron as the base. That means it can serve double-duty as a great griddle! Turn it upside down and place it on a lid stand. It is slightly concave so you can easily cook without having your ingredients run off. Place your coals underneath and use it to fry eggs, griddle cakes, or sausages.

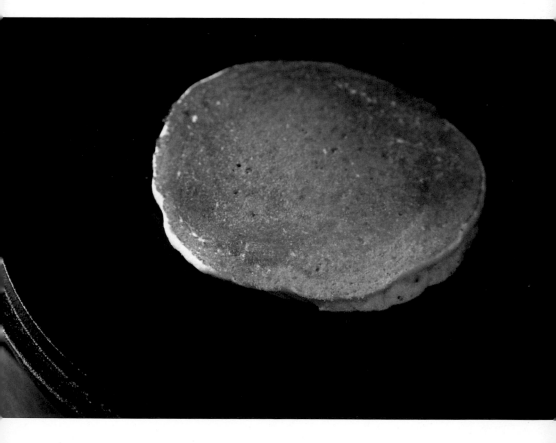

USE PARCHMENT LINERS

Parchment liners are a lifesaver for baking or cooking recipes that are high in sugar content, as well as cakes and breads that need to be pulled fully formed from the oven. I use Coleman Dutch Oven Parchment Liners. They are 20 in. (50.8 cm) round, so they can be used in most Dutch oven sizes.

CONSIDER CAKE PAN LINERS

Some people are big fans of placing whole cake pans inside their Dutch oven. They work well for baked products and do save your Dutch oven surface from possible damage from high-acid ingredients or tough-to-clean beans. But they do reduce the capacity of your oven considerably and I prefer the results I get from my food actually coming in contact with the oven's surface.

BRING A BLOWTORCH

No, I don't mean the giant industrial size that you buy to cut metal. A small culinary blowtorch has become a regular part of our gear. We use it to finish off a crunchy crust or to add a caramelized topping to a dessert.

REMOVE YOUR FOOD TO STOP THE COOKING PROCESS

Some recipes can simmer happily for a long time. It is always nice to see an oven filled with stew waiting for folks to arrive into camp. But keep in mind that Dutch ovens stay hot for a long time. Even after they are removed from their heat source, the temperature inside is still high. So if your recipe is done, remove your food immediately!

KEEP IT CLEAN

The inside surface of your Dutch oven is where the magic happens. And it doesn't ask for much to keep performing perfectly year after year. Maintain it properly and it truly will last forever.

Some foods are hard on the surface of your Dutch oven. Sweet, sugary foods can be really hard to clean off and high-acid food can eat away at the surface. Some

people place cake pans right into their ovens to avoid these problems. For baking, I am a big fan of parchment liners. They keep your oven perfectly clean and allow you to lift the food out very easily. As for high-acid foods like chili or spaghetti sauce, I don't worry too much. The key is to remove the food after cooking (never store your leftovers in the Dutch oven), and then clean and oil it properly afterward.

If you have stubborn, stuck food, add 2 or 3 in. (5 or 8 cm) of water to the oven and put it back on the coals to boil for a few minutes. That should be enough to loosen the worst of it.

I NEVER clean my Dutch oven with detergent. I use a handful of coarse salt to clean mine. In the field, half a cut potato works well for scrubbing the salt. If you use a scrubber, make it one of those soft plastic ones. I keep a plastic putty knife in my kit for scraping stubborn bits of food. Dry your oven immediately after cleaning it. Lightly oil the inside surface with vegetable oil before putting it away. And don't forget your lid. The Dutch oven lid captures all the condensation, so even though it may not need cleaning, it usually needs to be dried and oiled before being put away.

DON'T MIX HOT AND COLD

Ice-cold water can crack a hot oven, and hot ingredients can damage a cold oven, so introduce temperatures gently. Never try to clean a hot oven right away. Always give it time to cool before you start scrubbing.

SEASON WELL!

Most cast-iron Dutch ovens on the market today come pre-seasoned. The good news is that many of the fats and oils you use in your Dutch oven help to keep the condition of the cast iron in good shape. But some ingredients, such as beans and high-acid vegetables like tomatoes, can damage that beautiful coating. You may notice uneven marks inside the oven or find that food is suddenly sticking to the surface. If you put your oven away without thoroughly drying it, it may even start to show spots of rust.

To re-season your oven (or to season an unseasoned oven) scrub it down thoroughly, making sure to eliminate any signs of rust. Dry thoroughly with a soft cloth. Place it in a preheated 350°F (177°C) oven for 10 minutes or so to complete the drying process. Remove it from the oven.

Using oiled paper towels, coat the oven and the lid with oil inside and out. Place back in the oven upside down, placing a cookie sheet or layer of foil beneath it to catch dripping oil. Heat in the oven for one hour. Turn off your oven and let the Dutch oven cool inside, then remove it and wipe off any excess oil. Apply another light layer of oil all over the oven. It is now ready to use.

STORE YOUR OVEN PROPERLY

Your cast-iron Dutch oven is designed to last forever, but it pays to do the small amount of work needed to keep it in peak condition.

I oil my Dutch oven after every use, usually using vegetable or olive oil. This works well for ovens that are used often, as mine are. But if you use your Dutch oven primarily for the occasional camping trip, I suggest that you use mineral oil before storing it. Unlike vegetable oils that may turn rancid over time, mineral oil will provide a safe seal for your out-of-season oven. Make sure your oven is thoroughly dry. If it isn't, heat it in the oven for a few minutes to evaporate the last of the moisture. Then coat inside and out of the oven and lid with a light layer and wipe off any excess.

Store your oven with the lid slightly ajar so that air can circulate. Cover it and keep in a dry location—basements and garages may expose the oven to too much humidity that can start rusting out your oven.

CHAPTER 2

Heating Your Dutch Oven

The Dutch oven is a fryer-broiler-stewer-roaster-steamer-baking oven all in one. It is designed to keep moisture in and retain and circulate heat directly around your food. On top of that, if you take good care of it, it will last forever! Learn how to heat it properly so that you can get the most out of its versatility.

Part of the fun of outdoor cooking is that, well, you are outside. But whether you are camping in a national park, setting up a picnic streamside, or cooking in your own backyard, outdoor cooking also brings with it a number of factors that have to be considered. Wind, air temperature, humidity, location, and your cooking surface all play a part in how you will generate and maintain your heat. A little wind can gobble up your coals faster than you had planned, high humidity can slow them down, and a shady location or cold ground surface can lower your temperature by 25°F (15°C) or more.

Lodge Manufacturing has an excellent chart that tells you exactly how many briquettes to use for various temperatures. This chart is a great starting point, and with time you will learn how to make adjustments based on your conditions.

Temperature Desired (°F)

Oven Size		325	350	375	400	425	450
8"	Total Briquettes	15	16	17	18	19	20
	Top/Bottom	$^{10}/_5$	$^{11}/_5$	$^{11}/_6$	$^{12}/_6$	$^{13}/_6$	$^{14}/_6$
10"	Total Briquettes	19	21	23	25	27	29
	Top/Bottom	$^{13}/_6$	$^{14}/_7$	$^{16}/_7$	$^{17}/_8$	$^{18}/_9$	$^{19}/_{10}$
12"	Total Briquettes	23	25	27	29	31	33
	Top/Bottom	$^{16}/_7$	$^{17}/_8$	$^{18}/_9$	$^{19}/_{10}$	$^{21}/_{10}$	$^{22}/_{11}$
14"	Total Briquettes	30	32	34	36	38	40
	Top/Bottom	$^{20}/_{10}$	$^{21}/_{11}$	$^{22}/_{12}$	$^{24}/_{12}$	$^{25}/_{13}$	$^{26}/_{14}$
16"	Total Briquettes	37	39	41	43	45	47
	Top/Bottom	$^{25}/_{12}$	$^{26}/_{13}$	$^{27}/_{14}$	$^{28}/_{15}$	$^{29}/_{16}$	$^{30}/_{17}$

Table courtesy of Lodge Manufacturing Company

CALCULATING HEAT

Because the Dutch oven is such a versatile cooking unit, it only makes sense that there are a number of ways to heat and cook with it. That's why I tend to calculate my coal needs myself, based on a few basic rules.

A single charcoal briquette generates around 15°F (10°C). That means that to maintain a temperature of about 350°F (177°C), you would use approximately 24 coals. This is handy to know, but not entirely reliable because it doesn't factor in oven size or other conditions. It is just a good starting point.

It is always best to be a little conservative when starting out. An overly hot oven can burn your food. It is always easier to build the heat than it is to cool down a hot Dutch oven.

COOKING METHODS

Laying coals for different types of cooking is a matter of ratios. The first number always refers to the coals you will put on top of your oven. The second number is the number of coals you will put on the bottom. For example, 4:1 means 4 times as many coals on the *top* of the oven as on the bottom. On the

other hand, 1:4 means that there would be 4 times as many coals on the *bottom* as on the top.

Boiling and Frying

These are the most basic methods for cooking with your Dutch oven because all the heat is underneath. The temperature is kept high for the entire cooking process. This is the one time that you would use an entire spread of charcoal as your heat source. A spread is a single layer of coals placed directly under the oven. There is no need to produce a huge mound of charcoal—too much heat can actually harm the oven.

Simmering and Stewing

We use this method for soups, stews, and other recipes that require slow simmering. The primary heat source is underneath the oven, with a few coals on top to keep everything warm. A ratio of 1:4 is about right for simmering.

Stewing and simmering does not call for sophisticated calculations, just a bit of common sense. A few coals on top will help the entire oven stay warm. Start with 8 coals on the bottom and 2 on the lid for a 12 in. (30.5 cm) Dutch oven, and adjust your temperature up or down by adding or removing coals.

Roasting

Meats are generally cooked using even heat. For roasting, we use a 1:1 ratio. That means that the heat source is evenly distributed on the top and the bottom of the oven.

To start, take your oven size and double it to get the total number of coals needed. For example, a 12 in. (30.5 cm) oven would require 24 coals. Place 12 coals on top and 12 on the bottom to maintain a 350°F temperature.

Baking

While roasting is somewhat forgiving, baked recipes call for a little more precision. Baking requires more heat on top of the oven than on the bottom to keep the bottom from burning and to ensure even cooking on top. For baking, we use something closer to a 3:1 ratio. A quick way to calculate the right number of coals is the 3 up/3 down rule.

Step 1	Start with the diameter of your Dutch oven.	12 in. (30.5 cm) oven
Step 2	For your top heat, add 3 to the diameter of your oven.	15 top coals
Step 3	For your bottom heat, subtract 3 from the diameter of your oven.	9 bottom coals

CHAPTER 3

Breakfast

I have to admit that I am not the first one out of the sleeping bag in the morning, particularly if the temperature is cool. Fortunately, Jim is always happy to brave the weather to get the coffee on and prepare the coals. Jim is the master of brewing "Norwegian coffee," a recipe we brought with us from northern Wisconsin. Although not a Dutch oven recipe, it is ideal for camp.

Fill a pot with 10 cups (1 L) of water and bring to a boil. In a bowl, combine 10 tablespoons coffee grounds, 1 egg, and ¼ cup (25 mL) of water. Stir the egg and coffee mixture into the boiling water and continue to boil for 2–3 minutes. Before serving, remove from heat and add 1 cup (100 mL) of cold water. This settles the coffee grounds to the bottom of the pot. Pour a cup, using a strainer if you prefer your coffee without any floating debris. Add milk and sugar and bring to your wife in her sleeping bag!

Why eggs, you ask? I am not sure, although I do know the egg adds body to the coffee and helps to remove any bitterness, leaving you with a smooth, mild cup.

In spite of my reluctance for early mornings, I do love breakfast. Because we are often getting ready to dash off on some adventure, the lid of the Dutch oven is often our tool of choice. Just flip it upside down and place on a small spread of coals for a quick fry-up of eggs and fried bread or pancakes. But when the day calls for a leisurely morning at camp, I love to make large Dutch oven breakfasts.

When our girls were young, we spent several weeks in the Wind River Range, camping at the base of Square Top Mountain. It was a real luxury to set up a camp kitchen for an extended stay, and I got to experiment with a range of ingredients and cooking styles. With three adults and two children a captive audience to my attempts, I developed a number of recipes that stay with us to this day.

DUTCH'S LAYERED POTATO CASSEROLE

What started out as a way to use leftovers has turned into a favorite camp breakfast. Substitute the ham for cooked, crumbled sausage if you prefer.

2 tablespoons (30 g) butter
2 tablespoons (12 g) flour
1 cup (240 mL) milk
2 cups (240 g) cheddar cheese, grated
¼ teaspoon (1.25 g) salt
¼ teaspoon (1.25 g) cayenne
¼ teaspoon (1.25 g) black pepper
4 large red potatoes, scrubbed and sliced thin
1 small onion, diced
4 hard-boiled eggs
½ pound (.25 kg) cooked ham, diced
½ cup (60 g) bread crumbs
1 tablespoon (15 g) butter

Make a cheese sauce by melting butter in a saucepan. Stir in flour and blend. Add milk and stir constantly until sauce is thick. Stir in cheese and stir until blended. Add salt, cayenne, and black pepper.

Remove sauce from heat.

Layer half the potatoes, onion, eggs, ham, and sauce into a 10 in. (25.5 cm) Dutch oven. Repeat layers, ending with sauce on top. Top with bread crumbs and dabs of butter. Bake at 350°F (177°C) for 35 minutes.

OVERNIGHT BREAKFAST CASSEROLE

Make this up the night before so all the ingredients can soak together. Pour it into a parchment-lined Dutch oven the next morning and bake.

12 eggs, beaten
10 slices bread, crusts removed and cubed
3 tablespoons (45 g) butter
3 cups (720 mL) milk
6 green onions, chopped
2 pounds (1 kg) pork sausage, cooked and crumbled
2 cups (240 g) cheddar cheese, grated
1 teaspoon (5 g) salt
¼ teaspoon (1.25 g) black pepper

Blend all ingredients and refrigerate overnight. In the morning, pour into 12 in. (30.5 cm) Dutch oven and bake at 350°F (177°C) for about an hour.

CARAMELIZED OVEN FRENCH TOAST

My kids' all-time favorite breakfast and the one they clamber for after a morning of cross-country skiing.

4 eggs
1½ cups (350 mL) milk
2 tablespoons (16 g) sugar
1 teaspoon (5 mL) vanilla
¼ teaspoon (1.25 g) salt
2 tablespoons (30 mL) corn syrup
½ cup (115 g) butter
1 cup (130 g) brown sugar
5 cups (300 g) bread cubes

In a bowl, beat together eggs, milk, sugar, vanilla, and salt. Set aside.

Line 10 in. (25.5 cm) Dutch oven with parchment and place over heat. Into the warm Dutch oven, place the corn syrup, butter, and brown sugar, stirring to combine as the butter melts. Add bread cubes. Pour egg mixture over bread. Dot with butter and let stand for 10 minutes.

Bake at 350°F (177°C) for about 45 minutes. Flip onto a plate and serve hot with butter and sausages.

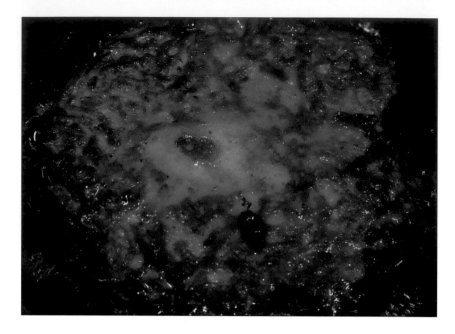

HASHED POTATO HASH

A warm tummy-filler on a chilly morning—two fried eggs on top completes the perfect hearty breakfast.

1 pound (.45 kg) bacon
½ cup (75 g) green pepper, diced
½ cup (75 g) onion, diced
4–5 cups (.8–1 kg) shredded hash brown potatoes
1 (10½-ounce) (310-mL) can cream of mushroom soup
Salt and pepper to taste
1 cup (120 g) cheddar cheese, grated

Cook bacon until crisp. Remove bacon from oven and set aside to cool. When it is cooled, crumble it. Add peppers and onions to bacon fat and cook until tender. Add potatoes, crumbled bacon, and mushroom soup to pot and mix thoroughly. Season with salt and pepper. Cover and bake at 350°F (177°C) for 30 minutes or until potatoes are browned. Sprinkle cheese on top and cook covered another 5 minutes or until melted.

CHERRY CRUMBLE COFFEE CAKE

As much as I love fresh fruit, I have a secret weakness for cherry pie filling. This decadent breakfast pastry is a perfect lazy Sunday morning treat at camp.

1 package refrigerated crescent sheet dough
8 ounces (227 g) cream cheese, softened

½ cup (50 g) powdered sugar

1 egg

1 (21-ounce) (595-g) can cherry pie filling

½ cup (115 g) butter

1 cup (200 g) brown sugar

¾ cup (75 g) flour

¾ cup (60 g) oatmeal

Butter a 10 in. (25.5 cm) Dutch oven and layer the bottom with the crescent roll dough. Blend the cream cheese, powdered sugar, and egg until smooth, and spread over the dough. Spoon the cherry pie filling on top. Make a crumble of butter, brown sugar, flour, and oatmeal, and cover the cherries with it. Cover and bake at 350°F (177°C) for 30–35 minutes. If your crust is done, but the crumble isn't brown enough, stack more coals on top for an additional 5 minutes or brown crumble topping with a culinary blowtorch.

CHEESE STRATA

A great way to use day-old bread. There are lots of variations on this recipe; I sometimes add ham or bacon, or even a handful of spinach.

8 cups (475 g) bread, cut into 1 in. (2.54 cm) cubes

2 cups (240 g) cheddar cheese, grated

8 eggs, beaten

4 cups (950 mL) milk

1 teaspoon (2.4 g) dry mustard

1 teaspoon (5 g) salt
1 teaspoon (5 g) black pepper
2 teaspoons (10 mL) Worcestershire sauce

Line 10 in. (25.5 cm) Dutch oven with parchment. Add bread and cheese. Blend eggs, milk, and seasonings and pour over bread and cheese. Bake at 350°F (177°C) for 1 hour or until center is soft but set.

JALAPEÑO AND HAM QUICHE

This is a favorite quiche recipe—smoky with a bit of heat. But any quiche recipe will work just as well in the Dutch oven.

1 packaged pie crust
1 cup (220 g) ham, diced
½ cup (75 g) onion, chopped
1 medium tomato, chopped and seeded
2 jalapeño peppers, seeds removed and chopped
½ cup (37 g) mushrooms, chopped
2 cups (260 g) Monterey Jack cheese, shredded
8 eggs, beaten
1 cup (236 mL) milk
1 cup (242 g) sour cream
½ teaspoon (1.2 g) dry mustard

Roll out the pie crust and arrange it on center of parchment paper. Place in bottom of 10 in. (25.5 cm) Dutch oven and up the sides about 2 in. (5 cm). Place ham, onion, tomato, peppers, mushrooms, and cheese in the crust. Combine eggs, milk, sour cream, and dry mustard and pour over the other ingredients, being careful not to spill the eggs over the sides of the crust. Bake at 350°F (177°C) for 30–35 minutes or until the center is set.

BISCUITS AND GRAVY

My guilty pleasure is not cookies or pie—it's biscuits and gravy. And it never tastes better than outdoors on a cool fall day.

1 pound (453 g) ground pork sausage
2–4 tablespoons (15–30 g) flour
6 cups (1.4 L) milk
Salt
Pepper

Fry sausage in Dutch oven until completely cooked. Remove cooked sausage from Dutch oven with a slotted spoon. Over low heat, add flour into sausage drippings, stirring until bubbly. Add milk, and continue to stir until thickened. Add sausage back into pot. Season as desired. Serve over fresh biscuits (see page 54).

BREAKFAST PIZZA WITH HAM AND BRAISED ONIONS

More rustic than a quiche, this variation on pizza combines a thick biscuit crust with a topping of hearty ingredients and melted cheese.

1 biscuit recipe, homemade or packaged tube
4 ounces (113 g) ham

½ cup (75 g) braised onions, chopped

2 cups (60 g) chopped spinach

3 eggs

¼ cup (60 mL) milk

Salt and pepper

⅔ cup (80 g) mild cheddar cheese

Preheat 10 in. (25.5 cm) Dutch oven and lid. Roll out biscuit dough to about 12 in. (30.5 cm) on a parchment circle. Lift the parchment and dough, and place it in Dutch oven, arranging dough so there is a nice edge all around. Sprinkle ham and braised onions evenly over dough and top with chopped spinach. Beat together eggs, milk, salt, and pepper, and pour over the top of the pizza. Top with cheese. Cover and bake at 350°F (177°C) for 25 minutes or until eggs are set.

Southwestern variation: Use crumbled sausage, bell peppers, and onions in place of ham, braised onions, and spinach. Top with Monterey Jack cheese. Serve with salsa.

DUANE'S BIG BURRITO BREAKFAST

Simple, hearty, and easily adaptable to your favorite ingredients. Use ham instead of sausage, or add a can of black beans and a cup of diced tomatoes.

1 large onion, chopped

1 large green pepper, chopped

2 tablespoons (30 mL) oil

1 pound (453 g) ground pork sausage

15 eggs, beaten and seasoned with salt and pepper

12 tortillas

Salsa

Grated cheese

Avocados

Sour cream

Sauté onion and green pepper in oil until softened. Add sausage and cook until crumbly. Stir in the eggs and simmer until they are set. Place stack of tortillas on top of the eggs. Cover and bake at 325°F (163°C) for about 5–7 minutes, or until tortillas are soft and warm. Remove tortillas and serve with eggs, salsa, grated cheese, avocados, and sour cream.

CLASSIC SOUTHERN HOECAKES

There are many interpretations of the hoecake; some are made using fresh corn and no added sugar. This recipe is essentially a cornmeal pancake, but with more flavor and texture than a standard pancake. I like them served in the style of the South: with fresh country butter and sorghum molasses.

1 cup (170 g) cornmeal

1 cup (100 g) flour

⅓ cup (65 g) sugar

1 teaspoon (5 g) salt

1 teaspoon (5 g) baking soda

1¼ cups (295 mL) buttermilk

2 tablespoons (30 mL) vegetable oil or melted butter

2 eggs, beaten

Mix cornmeal, flour, sugar, salt, and baking soda. Add buttermilk, oil, and eggs, and stir to blend. Place the Dutch oven lid upside down on coals and grease lightly with vegetable oil. Drop ¼ cup (60 g) of batter onto the hot surface, swirling it with the back of the spoon to make a nice round cake. Cook until surface bubbles, then flip over to cook the other side. Serve with butter and syrup.

MR. KLING'S POTATO DOUGHNUTS

Growing up, I always looked forward to the day my neighbor would make his unbelievable potato doughnuts. He never forgot me—within moments of them coming out of his fryer, I always had my own special bag. I don't like to fry at home in the kitchen, but we love to make them outside. To me, they are perfect unadorned, but sprinkle with cinnamon or powdered sugar if you like.

1½ cups (195 g) sugar
⅓ cup (78 g) shortening
6 eggs, beaten
2 cups (420 g) mashed potatoes
5¼ cups (550 g) flour
8 teaspoons (30 g) baking powder
2 teaspoons (10 g) salt
½ teaspoon (1.25 g) nutmeg
½ teaspoon (1.25 g) cinnamon
Oil, for frying

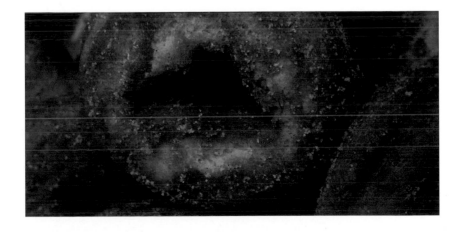

Beat together sugar, shortening, and eggs. Stir in mashed potatoes. Blend flour, baking powder, salt, and spices together. Gradually add the flour mixture to blend. Refrigerate overnight.

Roll dough out and cut with a doughnut cutter. Drop a few at a time into a few inches of hot oil, being careful not to let them touch. Turn doughnut once and brown other side. Lift from oil and drain on paper towels.

CHAPTER 4

Breads

Simple bread recipes are a great way to experiment with your heating skills. The ingredients are relatively inexpensive and there is usually someone around to help eat your mistakes, especially if you have some good butter and a pot of jam handy.

When I was learning to bake, I cooked cornbread after cornbread after cornbread, burning some and undercooking others, until my family begged me to stop. After a while, the birds and squirrels noticed something was up, and came to share in the spoils of my labor. I think everyone was relieved to have a few extra mouths to help with the testing.

Baking relies on the proper coal ratios. Start with approximately 3 coals on top for every 1 below. Though not an exact formula, for a 10 in. (25.5 cm) Dutch oven, I would start with about 20 coals, placing 14 coals on top and 6 on the bottom. Good top heat is crucial—too little and you end up with soggy, undercooked dough. Always preheat your lid to get the baking process off to a good start. While the oven itself is snuggled on its coals, the top of the oven has to do battle with the air temperature and the breezes to stay nice and warm. A properly preheated lid and shelter from the wind will help to ensure baking success.

I almost always line my Dutch oven with parchment paper for baking breads. For biscuits, rolls, pizza, and other firm dough, I assemble my recipe right on the parchment paper so that I can quickly lower the whole thing into the Dutch oven. This prevents my lid from cooling while I fuss with assembly. You can do the same thing for your batter breads, but assemble in a cake pan or bowl to keep the batter from running off before you have a chance to lift it into the oven.

After baking, parchment liners allow you to quickly lift your bread intact from the oven. This is very important because bread left in the Dutch oven continues to cook, even after it has been removed from the heat.

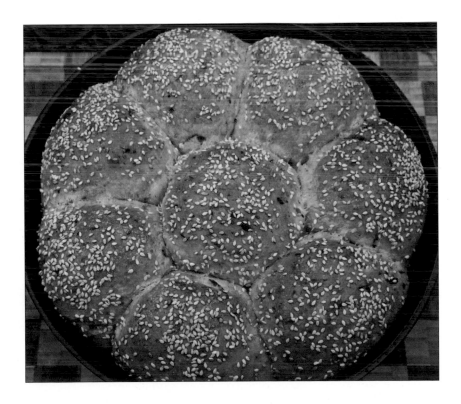

Of course, my favorite thing about parchment is the fact that there is no cleanup!

BAKING POWDER BISCUITS

This is the classic Southern biscuit—made with buttermilk instead of plain milk.

2 cups (200 g) flour
4 teaspoons (15 g) baking powder
¼ teaspoon (1 g) baking soda
¾ teaspoon (3.75 g) salt
½ cup (115 g) shortening
1½ cups (355 mL) buttermilk

Mix flour, baking powder, baking soda, and salt in a bowl. Add shortening, using a fork to cut it into the flour until you have the consistency of dry crumbs. Add buttermilk a little at a time, stirring gently until dough starts to pull away from bowl and forms a ball. Turn out of bowl and knead lightly a few times. Roll out to ½ in. (1.25 cm) thickness and cut with 2 in. (5.0 cm) biscuit cutter. Place the biscuits in a preheated 10 in. (25.5 cm) Dutch oven and bake at 350°F (177°C) for about 10–12 minutes.

CARMEN'S CORNBREAD

A simple recipe that makes consistently good bread. If you don't have buttermilk, just add 1 tablespoon (15 mL) of vinegar to the milk before using.

1½ cups (255 g) cornmeal
½ cup (50 g) flour
2 teaspoons (7.5 g) baking powder
1 teaspoon (5 g) sugar
1 teaspoon (5 g) salt

½ teaspoon (2 g) baking soda
¼ cup (60 g) bacon fat, butter, or shortening
1½ cups (355 mL) buttermilk
2 eggs

Beat all ingredients together and pour into 10 in. (25.5 cm) preheated Dutch oven. Bake at 350°F (177°C) for about 25 minutes.

ZUCCHINI CROWN ROLLS

Zucchini and cheese make these rolls stay fresh longer. That can be a good thing at camp, although they are so good they rarely make it past the first day. Make sure there is plenty of headroom in the oven because the bread needs room to crown.

2 cups (300 g) zucchini, grated
Salt
5 cups (500 g) flour
1 package yeast
¼ cup (45 g) freshly grated Parmesan cheese
1 teaspoon (5 g) salt
1 teaspoon (5 g) black pepper
2 tablespoons (30 mL) olive oil
About 2 cups (475 mL) lukewarm water
Milk and sesame seeds for glaze

Grate zucchini and sprinkle lightly with salt. Place in a colander to drain for about 30 minutes. Squeeze thoroughly and pat dry to remove excess moisture.

Mix the flour, yeast, Parmesan, salt, and black pepper together. Mix in the oil and zucchini. Stir in 1 cup water, and then add remaining water a little at a time, stirring until your dough is firm. Turn dough out of bowl and knead lightly, dusting with flour as needed. Place ball of dough in an oiled mixing bowl, turning it once to oil the top of dough. Cover with a towel and set in a sunny place to rise. Dough should double in size. Time for rising will vary. On a warm, sunny day, less than an hour should do it.

Punch down dough and knead it lightly. Cut into 8 equal pieces, rolling each into a ball. Place balls into a parchment-lined 12 in. (30.5 cm) Dutch oven. Brush the tops with milk and sprinkle with sesame seeds. Cover with a towel and let rise about 30 minutes.

Bake at 350°F (177°C) for 35–40 minutes.

TOBY'S TEX MEX CORNBREAD

My friend Toby shared this recipe years ago, and it remains one of our favorites. Moist and packed with flavor, it's almost a meal in itself

1½ cups (255 g) cornmeal
1 cup (236 mL) milk
¾ teaspoon (3.75 g) salt
½ cup (115 g) melted butter
½ teaspoon (2 g) baking soda
1 (14-ounce) (420 mL) can cream-style corn
½ pound (225 g) Monterey Jack cheese, grated
6 green onions, whites and greens diced
1 (4-ounce) (120-mL) can diced green chilies

Mix cornmeal, milk, salt, butter, baking soda, and canned corn together. Pour half the batter into a 10 in. (25.5 cm) Dutch oven. Layer the cheese, onions, and green chilies over the batter. Pour the rest of the batter on top. Bake at 350°F (177°C) for 35–40 minutes.

BANANA BREAD

Easy and delicious—the first bread I ever baked in the Dutch oven.

⅓ cup (78 g) melted butter
3 ripe bananas, smashed
1 cup (130 g) brown sugar
1 egg
1 teaspoon (5 mL) vanilla
1 teaspoon (4 g) cardamom
1 teaspoon (4 g) baking soda
Pinch of salt
1½ cups (150 g) flour

Mix butter with the smashed bananas in a large mixing bowl. Add in the brown sugar, egg, and vanilla. Stir the cardamom, baking soda, salt, and flour into the wet mix. Pour mixture into a 10 in. (25.5 cm) Dutch oven. Bake at 350°F (177°C) for about 20 minutes or until a toothpick comes out clean.

SODA BREAD

This traditional Irish bread was originally cooked in a Dutch oven nestled into the fireplace. Baking soda is the only leavening agent, and it needs the acidity of the buttermilk to help activate it. The secret to success is to treat the dough gently, allowing the fragile CO_2 bubbles to do their job of creating a light loaf. Add ½ cup (75 g) raisins to make a version known as "Spotted Dog."

3½ cups (350 g) flour
1 teaspoon (5 g) sugar
1 teaspoon (5 g) salt
1 teaspoon (4 g) baking soda
1 cup (236 mL) buttermilk

Mix flour, sugar, salt, and baking soda together in a bowl to thoroughly combine. Add buttermilk a little at a time and continue to stir until a soft dough forms. Turn out onto a lightly floured board and knead very lightly. Form the dough into a round dome. With a sharp knife, cut a cross on the top of the circle and about halfway down the sides. Lift gently and place into a preheated Dutch oven. Cover and bake at 350°F (177°C) for 35 minutes. To test doneness, pick up the loaf and tap the bottom. It should sound a little hollow. For a softer crust, wrap in a towel to cool.

HUSH PUPPIES

For us, it's not a fish fry without hush puppies, but they also make the perfect accompaniment to down-home barbecue.

2¼ cups (383 g) cornmeal
2–3 tablespoons (30 g) onion, diced
1 teaspoon (5 g) sugar
¾ teaspoon (3 g) baking soda
1 teaspoon (5 g) salt
1½ cups (355 mL) buttermilk
Oil for frying

Mix cornmeal, onion, sugar, baking soda, and salt in a bowl. Add buttermilk to blend. Place about 1 in. (2.54 cm) of oil into Dutch oven and heat. Drop spoonfuls of dough into hot oil and fry until golden brown.

CRANBERRY-HAZELNUT MONKEY BREAD

If you want an easy morning, make the dough the night before and refrigerate after kneading. In the morning, just set dough in a warm place to rise before rolling into balls. For an even easier morning, use tubed biscuits instead of dough from scratch. This is a fun breakfast recipe, especially if you have kids to help roll the dough.

1 package active dry yeast
½ cup (118 mL) warm water
½ cup (118 mL) lukewarm milk

⅓ cup (44 g) sugar

⅓ cup (78 g) butter

1 teaspoon (5 g) salt

1 egg

3½–4 cups (350 g) flour

½ cup (95 g) sugar

2 tablespoons (15 g) cinnamon

½ cup (85 g) hazelnuts

½ cup (50 g) dried cranberries

12 tablespoons (172 g) butter

1 cup (225 g) packed brown sugar

Dissolve yeast in warm water. Stir in milk, sugar, butter, salt, egg, and 2 cups (200 g) flour. Beat until smooth. Continue to mix in flour until dough is ready to knead. Turn onto floured surface and knead until smooth and elastic. Place in oiled bowl, turning once to grease both sides. Cover and let rise in a warm place until doubled, about an hour and a half.

Mix white sugar and cinnamon in a small bowl. Punch down dough and pinch off 1 in. (2.54 cm) pieces, rolling each into a ball and then rolling in the sugar mixture to coat. Place balls into a parchment-lined 10 in. (25.5 cm) Dutch oven, layering until all dough is used. Add nuts and cranberries as you layer so they are dispersed throughout bread.

In a small pan, melt butter and brown sugar, stirring and boiling for about a minute. Pour over the dough. Bake at 350°F (177°C) for 35 minutes. When done, remove immediately and let cool for 10 minutes. Pull apart to eat.

YORKSHIRE PUDDING

This simplest possible bread is a traditional British accompaniment for roast beef. But it is perfect for any meal that leaves behind a layer of delicious drippings.

2 eggs
1 cup (210 g) flour
1 cup (236 mL) milk
½ teaspoon (2.5 g) salt
Butter

Beat eggs slightly, and then add flour, milk, and salt, stirring just until smooth. Remove roast meat from Dutch oven and set aside to rest. Pour out excess juices, leaving some drippings in pot. Add butter to drippings to make about ½ cup (118 mL), heating to melt. Pour the batter into the hot pan and cover. Bake at 425°F (218°C) for about 35–40 minutes. Cut into squares and serve with beef and gravy.

DEEP-DISH DUTCH OVEN PIZZA

I like yeast-based crusts, so I usually bring premade dough along. You can buy premade dough or use the dough recipe included here.

Pizza dough (see page 66)
1 cup (250 mL) pizza sauce
Meat or vegetable toppings of your choice
1 pound (450 g) shredded mozzarella

Bring refrigerated dough to room temperature to make it easier to work with. Stretch out dough by hand, to about 1–2 in. (2.5–5.0 cm) bigger than bottom of a 12 in. (30.5 cm) Dutch oven.

Using a parchment liner to make removal easier, lay the dough into the Dutch oven, forming it to the bottom and sides. There should be at least ½ in. (1.25 cm) lip all around. Add tomato sauce, meat and vegetable toppings, and cheese. Place over hot coals and add coals to lid. Bake

at 350°F (177°C) for 25–30 minutes, rotating oven and lid half a turn halfway through.

PIZZA DOUGH

1 package active dry yeast

1 cup (236 mL) warm water

2 cups (200 g) bread flour

2 tablespoons (30 mL) olive oil

1 teaspoon (5 g) salt

2 teaspoons (10 g) sugar

In a small bowl, dissolve yeast in warm water. In a large bowl, combine bread flour, olive oil, salt, and sugar. Add the yeast mixture and stir to combine. Knead with hands until dough is stiff and a nice ball is formed. Cover and rise until doubled in volume, about 30 minutes.

Turn dough out onto a floured surface and roll it into a circle.

CHAPTER 5

Soups and Stews

My husband is not a big cook, but he does love his stews and chili. Jim is always willing to start dinner if it involves throwing together simple chunks of meat and potatoes, and maybe some tomatoes and onions. And it helps if there is some beer nearby. At camp, we are big believers in the tradition of "one for the pot and one for the chef."

You can turn your Dutch oven into the perfect slow cooker by hanging it over the campfire on a tripod. Hang your pot close to the coals for searing your meat, and then use the adjustable chain to raise your oven away from the direct heat to reduce the cooking temperature. Stews, soups, and sauces can all simmer away in this way—

perfect for keeping dinner hot for stragglers arriving back at camp after a long day's hunt.

Since you are suspending a pot of hot food on a chain, make sure you have a safe setup. Use a good quality tripod with strong, stable legs. Make sure your lid lifter is handy, and keep your leather gloves nearby.

BARTENDER'S CHILI

Got a cooler full of cold ones? Create a flavor bridge by adding beer to the pot, then serving the same beer with dinner. I like a dark stout in this recipe, but some say any beer will suffice. My friend Martha Greenlaw always adds dark rum too. I have taken up her habit—using a special Newfoundland rum called Screech.

1 tablespoon (15 mL) vegetable oil
3 pounds (1.3 kg) ground beef
1 large onion, coarsely chopped
2 red or yellow bell peppers, seeded, coarsely chopped
1 large jalapeño, chopped
2 cloves garlic, peeled and sliced
1 (28-ounce) (300-g) can crushed tomatoes
8 ounces (236 mL) tomato sauce
2 tablespoons (15 g) chili powder
¼ teaspoon (.5 g) cayenne pepper
1 tablespoon (12 g) sugar
1 tablespoon (12 g) salt
1(12-ounce) (355-mL) bottle Guinness or other stout
½ cup (236 mL) dark rum

2 (15-ounce) (300-g) cans
    black beans, drained and
    rinsed
Salt and pepper to taste
Cheddar cheese, grated
Green onions, chopped

Brown ground beef with oil in Dutch oven. Add onion, bell peppers, jalapeño, and garlic, and continue to cook, stirring occasionally until vegetables are tender. Add crushed tomatoes, tomato sauce, chili powder, cayenne, sugar, salt, beer, and rum. Simmer two hours. Drain black beans and rinse to remove excess starch. Add to the pot and continue to cook for 20 minutes to heat beans thoroughly. Adjust seasonings as needed. Garnish with grated cheddar cheese and chopped green onions.

GRINGO'S GARDEN CHILI VERDE

Tomatillos, jalapeños, and onions are core ingredients in our summer garden, so this chili is a big favorite at harvest time. If you use commercial green salsa in this recipe, add an extra jalapeño to the pot for a little more kick.

4 tablespoons (60 mL) oil
3 pounds (1.4 kg) lean pork, cut into ½ in. (1.25 cm) cubes
1 large white onion, chopped
4 cloves garlic, minced
1 jalapeño, chopped (optional)
2–3 cups (300–450 g) green salsa (store-bought or from
    recipe below)
1 (12-ounce) (354-mL) bottle of Mexican beer, such as
    Corona (use chicken stock if you prefer)
Salt and pepper to taste
Sour cream

Heat oil in 10 in. (25.5 cm) Dutch oven. Season cubed pork with salt and pepper and add to pot, stirring until meat is well browned. Add onion, garlic, and jalapeño to the pot, and sauté until vegetables are tender. Add green salsa and beer, and season to taste. Simmer for 2 hours. Serve with a dollop of sour cream.

FRESH GREEN SALSA

Tomatillos are fairly easy to grow, so if you have a garden, add them to your mix. This salsa is positively addictive. Make it as mild or as hot as you like. And make plenty—it's great with tortilla chips or served over enchiladas. I usually make this in batches at home with a food processor, but if you are at camp, just dice ingredients fine and combine.

1 pound (454 g) tomatillos, husks removed and cut into
 quarters
1 small white onion
3 cloves garlic, peeled
1 (4-ounce) (115-g) can chopped green chilies
½ cup (20 g) fresh cilantro
2 jalapeños, seeds removed
Juice of ½ lime
1 teaspoon (5 g) salt

In a food processor, combine all ingredients. Use the pulse setting to coarsely chop, stopping to scrape the bowl as needed. Store in refrigerator until ready to use.

CORN AND CHICKEN CHOWDER

Precooked chicken makes this chowder a quick and satisfying meal after a day on the river. Take the time to cut fresh corn kernels from the cob to make this chowder extra-special.

3 tablespoons (45 mL) vegetable oil
5 stalks celery, chopped
2 medium white onions, chopped
2 carrots, scrubbed and diced
5 medium red potatoes, scrubbed and diced

4 tablespoons (25 g) flour
2 cups (475 mL) milk
4 cups (945 mL) chicken stock
2 teaspoons (.5 g) herbes de Provence
4 cups (920 g) cooked chicken, diced
2 cups (300 g) fresh corn kernels
Salt and pepper

Heat the oil in a 12 in. (30.5 cm) Dutch oven. Add the celery, onions, and carrots. Sauté until onions are trans-

lucent, about 5 minutes. Add potatoes and cook another 10 minutes. Mix flour and milk to make a thin paste. Add the paste and the stock to the pot and bring to a boil. Add herbs and simmer until the potatoes and carrots are tender. Before serving, stir in chicken and fresh corn and heat through for about 5 minutes. Season with salt and pepper to taste.

CLASSIC BEAN SOUP

Beans, onions, and bacon are always a part of our camp pantry. Other vegetables are optional. Throw in whatever you have around.

1 cup (200 g) dried white beans
Water, for soaking
¼ pound (115 g) bacon, chopped
2 medium red potatoes, diced
2 carrots, diced
2 stalks celery, diced
1 medium onion, chopped
Salt and pepper

Soak the beans overnight. Drain and rinse. In the Dutch oven, fry chopped bacon until brown. Add beans, potatoes, carrots, celery, and onion. Add water to cover beans. Season with salt and pepper. Cover and simmer for 2 hours, checking now and then to adjust liquid.

THREE LITTLE PIGS LENTIL SOUP

The beauty of lentils is that no soaking is required, so they can be on the table in an hour. We like ours meaty, so we add three different types of pork to this recipe.

4 slices bacon, coarsely chopped
2 cups (450 g) ham, diced
12 ounces (340 g) kielbasa, sliced thick
1 large onion, chopped
1 large stalk celery, chopped (with green tops)
1 large carrot, chopped
1 potato, peeled and cut into large dice
1 clove garlic, peeled and diced
4 cups (946 mL) chicken stock
2 cups (400 g) dried lentils
1 bay leaf
1 teaspoon (1 g) fresh chopped thyme
Salt and pepper
1 large handful of fresh chopped spinach (optional)

Fry bacon in Dutch oven until just starting to brown. Add ham and kielbasa, and sauté for 5 minutes. Add onion, celery, carrot, potato, and garlic, and cook until vegetables start to soften. Stir in chicken stock, lentils, bay leaf, thyme, salt, and pepper. Cover and simmer for 1 hour. Before serving, stir in spinach and cook until wilted.

COOK'S CHOICE VEGETABLE BEEF SOUP

A vegetable beef soup designed to customize any way you wish. Start with the basic recipe and then add whatever else is on hand.

1 tablespoon (15 mL) vegetable oil
1 pound (454 g) beef chuck, cubed
2 cups (475 mL) beef stock
1 teaspoon (1 g) fresh chopped thyme, parsley, marjoram, or oregano, or a combination
1½ teaspoons (7.5 g) salt
¼ teaspoon (1.25 g) black pepper

2 carrots, peeled and sliced
1 large stalk celery, chopped
1 medium onion, chopped
1 (16-ounce) (454-g) can diced tomatoes
About 4 cups (945 mL) water

Other options to include:
1 potato, peeled and diced
½ cup (33 g) mushrooms, sliced
1 cup (150 g) green beans, cut into 1 in. (2.54 cm) lengths
½ cup (75 g) peas or sweet corn
1 cup (150 g) broccoli
½ cup (90 g) uncooked barley

Starch options:
1 cup (160 g) cooked elbow macaroni

1 cup (160 g) cooked rice

Handful of fresh chopped spinach

Place oil in Dutch oven. Add beef and sauté until brown. Stir in stock, herbs, salt, and pepper, and simmer until beef is tender, about 1½ hours.

Add the vegetables of your choice, along with canned tomatoes, and top with about 4 cups (945 mL) water. Cover and simmer another 45 minutes or until carrots are tender.

Before serving, add one of the starch options, if desired, and heat through. Stir in chopped spinach and cook until wilted.

BREAD SOUP

My husband loves tomato soup. I have never been a fan. But it was easy to agree on this version of the classic Italian bread soup, made with fresh tomatoes and leftover bread. We use fresh Roma tomatoes from the garden, but good canned Roma or plum tomatoes make a great substitute.

4 thick slices French bread
3 cloves garlic, peeled and sliced
1 medium onion, finely chopped
¼ cup (60 mL) olive oil
12 basil leaves, cut into chiffonades
2 pounds (900 g) Roma tomatoes, peeled and diced
4 cups (945 mL) chicken stock

1 teaspoon (5 g) salt
¼ teaspoon (1.25 g) black pepper
Parmesan cheese, grated

Place bread on grill over low coals. Don't toast them, just dry them out. Break bread into large pieces and set aside. Sauté the garlic and onion in olive oil until soft; be careful not to brown them.

Stack the basil leaves and roll them together, and then cut into thin slices to produce thin chiffonaded strips. Stir the basil and tomatoes into the Dutch oven with the garlic and onion and simmer for 15–20 minutes. Add chicken stock, bread, salt, and pepper, and continue to simmer for another 15–20 minutes. Stir occasionally to break down the bread and incorporate it into the broth. Sprinkle with freshly grated Parmesan cheese and serve.

BEEF AND STOUT STEW

Stout is a dark and toasty beer that creates a rich base for this otherwise basic stew. Use beef or your favorite game meat.

2 pounds (900 g) stew beef, cut into 1 in. (2.54 cm) chunks
3 tablespoons (45 g) flour
Salt and black pepper
3 tablespoons (45 mL) oil
1 large onion, chopped
2 cloves garlic, crushed

2 tablespoons (30 g) tomato paste

1 (12-ounce) (355-mL) bottle stout such as Guinness

3 carrots, cut into 1 in. (2.54 cm) chunks

4 red potatoes, quartered

8 ounces (75 g) mushrooms, halved

Toss beef with flour, and season with salt and pepper. Heat oil in Dutch oven and brown meat on all sides. Add the onion, cooking until it becomes softened. Stir in the crushed garlic, tomato paste, and beer. Add the carrots, potatoes, and mushrooms. Cover and simmer until the meat is tender, about 2 hours. Taste and adjust seasonings. Serve with crusty bread.

CHAPTER 6

Sides

It is a shame to refer to this section of recipes merely as "side dishes." It makes them sound like afterthoughts, when in fact they are often the stars of the meal. This section provides a selection of starches and vegetables, as well as sinfully delicious french fries, decadently cooked in duck fat.

One of the really fun ways to do your side dishes is to gather the ingredients yourself. In Maine, we can't wait for the fiddleheads to come out in the spring. We steam them for 7 or 8 minutes, and if we are feeling particularly decadent, we serve with hollandaise sauce for a taste that puts asparagus to shame. Morel and chanterelle mushrooms can be harvested from May into the summer.

(Those are the ones we know; in fact, there are hundreds of edible mushrooms. Just make sure you get some advice from an expert before experimenting.) We sauté them in olive oil with garlic, onion, and strong country ham. We add a handful of fresh herbs and simmer gently to wilt. Or we cook them in butter and finish with a bit of heavy cream, salt, and pepper.

SCALLOPED POTATOES

A camp basic that is hard to beat. Make your own variation by changing up the cheese or adding chunks of ham or sausage.

3 pounds (1.3 kg) scrubbed, unpeeled red potatoes, sliced thin
1 small onion, diced
2 cups (240 g) sharp cheddar cheese
4 tablespoons (60 g) butter
2 cups (475 mL) milk

Line 12 in. (30.5 cm) Dutch oven with parchment paper. Layer about half of the sliced potatoes and onion in the bottom. Sprinkle with 1 cup of cheese and season with salt and pepper and dots of butter. Repeat layers, ending with potatoes on top. Pour enough milk over the potatoes just to cover. Add more dots of butter. Cover and bake at 350°F (177°C) for 1 hour or until potatoes are tender.

BASIC RICE PILAF

There are endless variations of rice pilaf. This is the basic recipe, but don't be afraid to experiment by adding your favorite vegetables or herbs. I love the nuttiness of the brown and wild rice blend, but if you prefer to substitute long-grain white rice, reduce cooking time by about half.

3 tablespoons (45 mL) olive oil
1 medium onion, chopped

2 cups (300 g) blend of brown and wild rice
½ teaspoon (2.5 g) salt
4 cups (945 mL) chicken broth
Slivered almonds to garnish

Heat oil in 10 in. (25.5 cm) Dutch oven. Add onions and rice, stirring until onions are translucent and rice has a nice light toast color. Stir in salt. Add chicken broth and cover. Bake at 350°F (177°C) for an hour and 15 minutes or until rice is tender. Fluff rice and serve, garnished with slivered almonds.

Variation 1: To accompany beef or another dark meat, add ½ cup (40 g) chopped mushrooms when sautéing the onions. Use beef stock instead of chicken stock. Add 1 teaspoon (3 g) dried thyme.

Variation 2: For a fragrant Indian version, use chicken stock and add ½ teaspoon (2 g) allspice, ½ teaspoon (2 g) turmeric, and ¼ teaspoon (1 g) curry powder at the same time as the salt. Makes a beautiful yellow-colored side dish for chicken or fish.

DUCK FAT FRIES

Go ahead. You know you want to. These killer fries are so over-the-top good you won't be sorry, even if you have to hike that extra few miles the next day to burn them off.

Yukon Rose potatoes, scrubbed and skin on
Water
Salt

3 parts duck fat
7 parts cooking oil

Cut potatoes into fry strips. Put in a bowl and cover with cold salted water. Soak for a couple of hours.

Heat the duck fat and frying oil in the Dutch oven. Oil should be around 350°F (177°C), but I generally test by throwing in one fry. If it sizzles, the oil is probably ready.

Drain potatoes and pat dry. Add fries to the oil in small batches and cook for 5 minutes. Remove from pot and drain on paper towels. When they are all cooked, put them back into the oil for a second fry. Remove fries again, season with salt and pepper, and enjoy!

BROWNED POTATOES

A camp basic that we serve with almost everything.

½ pound (225 g) bacon, cut into 1 in. (2.54 cm) pieces
1 medium onion, chopped
1 small green pepper, diced
3 pounds (1.3 kg) red potatoes, skin on and cut into
    small chunks
Salt and pepper
½ cup (118 mL) water
2 tablespoons (30 g) butter, cut into small pieces

In a hot Dutch oven, cook bacon. Add onion and pepper, and cook until soft. Add potatoes to the pot, stirring to coat with bacon grease. Salt and pepper to taste. Add water to the bottom of the oven and dot with butter. Cover and cook about 30 minutes, or until potatoes are tender.

BAKED SQUASH

I can't wait until fall comes and the winter squash is ready. The Dutch oven is the perfect way to cook them. Sometimes I add halved apples to the pot. Baked squash and apples are the perfect side to a nice pork roast.

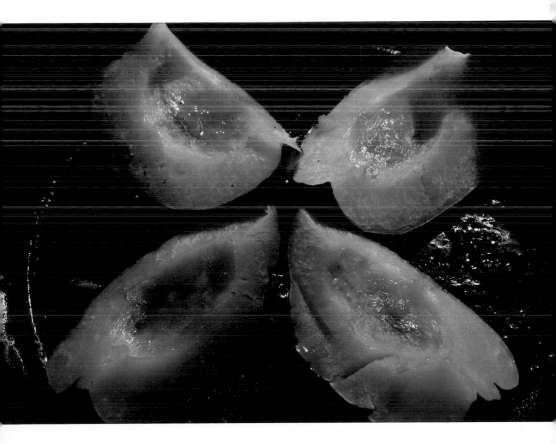

1 acorn squash
1 cup (236 mL) water
¼ cup (115 g) butter
½ cup (100 g) brown sugar

Cut the squash into quarters and remove the seeds. Place pieces cut side up in Dutch oven. Add 1 cup (236 mL) of water to the bottom of the pot. Place a pat of butter and 2 tablespoons (25 g) of brown sugar on each piece. Cover and bake at 350°F (177°C) for about an hour.

EASY HOPPIN' JOHN

Traditional Hoppin' John is simmered with a big ham hock and served over rice. This quicker one-pot version uses sausage to add the smoky flavor. Makes a substantial side dish with roasted chicken, or just add collard greens and cornbread to make a complete meal.

1 small onion, chopped
1 pound (454 g) kielbasa, sliced
2 tablespoons (30 mL) oil
1 small red pepper, chopped
3 (15-ounce) (1.3-kg) cans black-eyed peas, drained and
    rinsed
2½ cups (600 mL) chicken stock
¼ teaspoon (1 g) cayenne pepper
1 cup (236 mL) water
2 cups (57 g) uncooked instant rice

Sauté onion and kielbasa in oil until kielbasa starts to brown and onion softens. Stir in the red pepper, black-eyed peas, chicken stock, cayenne, and water, and bring to a boil. Add rice and cover. Bake at 350°F (177°C) until rice is tender, about 25–30 minutes.

MACARONI AND CHEESE

Simple and satisfying—and easy to adapt to any cheese you have along. A chunk of leftover Brie adds creaminess. Smoked Gouda produces a nice fragrant earthiness. Cleanup is a snap if you line the oven with parchment to bake

1½ cups uncooked elbow macaroni
1 small onion, chopped
¼ cup (60 g) butter
¼ cup flour
½ teaspoon (2.5 g) salt
¼ teaspoon (1.25 g) black pepper
1¾ cups (350 mL) milk
8 ounces (225 g) cheddar cheese, shredded
¼ cup (15 g) bread crumbs
¼ cup (45 g) Parmesan cheese, grated

Cook macaroni in boiling water until slightly firm. Drain and set aside. In a saucepan, sauté onion in butter until softened. Blend in flour, salt, and pepper. Stir and cook on low heat until mixture is smooth. Add milk, stirring to blend. Continue to cook and stir until a medium-consistency sauce is formed. Add cheese and stir until melted.

Place cooked macaroni in a parchment-lined 10 in. (25.5 cm) Dutch oven and pour cheese sauce over it, stirring to combine. Top with blend of bread crumbs and Parmesan. Cover and bake at 350°F (177°C) for about 30 minutes.

SWEET POTATO PANCAKE

1 large sweet potato, grated
½ medium onion, grated
¼ teaspoon (1.25 g) salt
¼ teaspoon (1.25 g) pepper
2 tablespoons (20 g) cornstarch
2 eggs
⅓ cup (80 mL) milk
Vegetable oil, for frying

Grate the sweet potato and onion together. Mix in salt, pepper, and cornstarch. Add eggs and milk; mix until combined.

Place ½ in. (.6 cm) of vegetable oil in the Dutch oven. Heat the oil to about 350°F (177°C). Spoon sweet potato mix into oven, spreading evenly with back of spoon. Cook for

a few minutes on each side, until nicely browned. Remove and let rest on a paper towel to drain off excess oil.

GREAT GREENS

1 smoked ham hock
10 cups (1 kg) collards, rib ends removed and torn into
coarse chunks
3 cups (700 mL) water
1¼ teaspoons (6.25 g) salt

Pack ingredients in a Dutch oven. Simmer for 2 or 3 hours. When you are ready to serve, remove hock from the oven, pull the meat off, and add back to the greens. Serve with Hot Pepper Vinegar (see page 96).

BRAISED ONIONS

Get your roast started and then place an oven containing these onions on top to simmer. A fantastically simple and delicious accompaniment to any kind of meat.

2 tablespoons (3 g) butter
2 tablespoons (3 mL) olive oil
4 large white onions, peeled and quartered
¼ cup (60 mL) beef broth
1¼ teaspoons (6.25 g) salt
½ teaspoon (2.5 g) black pepper
¼ cup (60 mL) bourbon

Heat butter and oil in Dutch oven. Add onions and toss to cover. Add beef broth and season with salt and pepper. Simmer on low coals or stack on top of oven containing roasting meat. Just before serving, add bourbon and continue to cook for another 3–5 minutes.

HOT PEPPER VINEGAR

I use this recipe for several things—marinating chicken, sprinkling on rice dishes, and serving with collard greens. A bottle of it is always a part of my pantry.

Fresh jalapeño peppers
White vinegar

Wash peppers and slice them in half, removing the seeds. Finely dice them and pack into a jar. Bring vinegar to a boil and pour over peppers, making sure peppers are completely covered. Add lid or cork to bottle and store in the refrigerator for a couple of weeks before using.

CHAPTER 7

Beef, Lamb, and Wild Game

My mother was a magician with meat. Her meats were always beautifully moist, perfectly seasoned, and unfailingly delicious. She was a culinary genius.

Or so I thought. As I got older and began to learn the secrets of Dutch oven cooking myself, I quickly realized that the talent I had attributed to my mother lay in large part directly at the feet of the Dutch oven itself.

Dutch ovens are uniquely qualified for roasting meat. The heavy cast iron gets very hot, allowing you to easily sear the meat on all sides. Iron conducts heat well so your roast cooks evenly. The tight-fitting lid keeps all the juices inside, delivering more flavor by circulating moisture constantly around the roast.

The good news is that roasted meats do not have to be high-end cuts. In fact, some of the best roasts are actually the less expensive, tougher cuts. Having a little more fat on them is an advantage, because slow cooking melts the fat and adds it to the pan juices gathering below. Look for nicely marbled shoulder roasts, chuck, or leg of lamb.

Season your roast with salt and pepper, garlic and herbs, or any type of rubbing concoction. Brown in oil at high heat, turning to sear on all sides. Your roast will spend most of its cooking time simmering in liquid, so this is the time to seal in the juices and develop the caramelized color and flavor that will help create your amazing pan juices.

Because your Dutch oven traps the juices, you don't need to add a lot of liquid to the bottom. A cup or two of wine or stock is fine if you would like to make gravy. If you are not concerned with sauce, even less is required.

After you sear your roast, pull off a few coals before settling it in to simmer. Roasts should not be cooked quickly; let them bubble along quietly at 300–325°F (148–163°C).

Pull your roast out of the oven and let it rest on a platter for a few minutes before serving. The advantages to this are twofold. First, your meat has time to settle and stop cooking, and second, you have time to finish off your sauce and get it ready to serve.

You too can be a culinary roast genius.

GOURMET POT ROAST

Wine, honey, and fresh thyme combine to create a rich, fragrant one-pot dinner that will call everyone to the fire.

Salt and pepper
3 tablespoons (45 mL) vegetable oil
4 pounds (1.8 kg) boneless beef chuck roast
2 small onions, quartered
3 carrots, cut into 2 in. (5.0 cm) chunks
1 cup (236 mL) beef stock

1 cup (236 mL) red wine

1 tablespoon (30 mL) honey

2 tablespoons (30 g) tomato paste

Bay leaf

6 sprigs fresh thyme

2 pounds (900 g) red potatoes

2 tablespoons (20 g) cornstarch

Season roast with salt and pepper. Heat oil in a 10 in. (25.5 cm) Dutch oven and brown the meat on all sides to seal in the juices. Add onions and carrots around the roast. Stir beef stock, red wine, honey, tomato paste, bay leaf, and fresh thyme together, and pour over the roast and vegetables.

Cover and bake at 325°F (163°C) for 2 hours, turning the roast over every 45 minutes or so.

Cut potatoes into quarters and arrange around the roast. Bake another 30 minutes or until the potatoes are tender. Remove meat and vegetables to serving platter.

Take ½ cup (118 mL) of juice from the pot and dissolve 2 tablespoons (20 g) cornstarch into it. Whisk the paste back into the pot, stirring until your gravy reaches the proper consistency. Remove from heat and serve with beef and vegetables.

SWISS STEAK

An old-fashioned classic, made better with the addition of bacon and red wine.

¼ cup (60 mL) vegetable oil or bacon drippings
2 pounds (900 g) round steak, cut into large chunks
Salt and pepper
¼ cup (25 g) flour
1 (14½-ounce) (410 g) can diced tomatoes
½ cup (118 mL) red wine
1½ cups (354 mL) beef broth
½ cup (75 g) onion, chopped
¼ cup (40 g) green bell pepper, chopped

2 stalks celery, chopped
¼ teaspoon (1 g) cayenne pepper

Heat bacon drippings or vegetable oil in Dutch oven. Season steak with salt and pepper, then dredge in flour. Place pieces in bacon drippings and sauté until brown. Add tomatoes, red wine, and beef broth to the pot, scraping brown bits from the bottom of the pan. Add onion, green pepper, and celery on top. Cover and simmer at 350°F (177°C) for two hours. Add cayenne to taste.

MUSTARD SHORT RIBS

Short ribs are so luxuriously rich, a small amount goes a long way. Serve these with mashed potatoes and steamed fiddleheads.

4 pounds (1.8 kg) beef short ribs, cut into 2 in. (5 cm) pieces
2 large onions, sliced
3 tablespoons (47 g) Dijon mustard
1 tablespoon (12 g) sugar
2 tablespoons (30 mL) lemon juice
3 cloves garlic, peeled and crushed
1 teaspoon (5 g) salt
½ teaspoon (2.5 g) black pepper
3 tablespoons (45 mL) vegetable oil

Place beef ribs and onions in a large, sealable plastic bag. Mix mustard, sugar, lemon juice, garlic, salt, and pepper. Pour into bag and seal, squeezing to coat ribs. Refrigerate overnight.

Pour oil into Dutch oven. Pull ribs out of the bag, setting aside onions and marinade, and place in oil. Cook over medium heat, turning to brown all sides.

Remove pot from heat and pour off all fat. Pour onions and marinade over ribs. Cover and bake at 325°F (163°C) for 2 hours.

BEEF AND BEAN CORNMEAL PIE

A warm, cozy casserole for a chilly day. Add a cup of shredded cheese on top for an extra treat.

2 cups (340 g) cornmeal
2 teaspoons (9 g) baking soda
1 teaspoon (5 g) salt
1 quart (946 mL) buttermilk
2 eggs, slightly beaten
4 tablespoons (60 mL) butter, melted

1 tablespoon (15 mL) vegetable oil
1 pound (450 g) ground beef
1 small onion, peeled and diced
1 clove garlic, peeled and minced
1 (10-ounce) (280-g) can pinto beans, drained and
    rinsed
1 (14½-ounce) (410-g) can diced tomatoes
1 cup (160 g) whole kernel corn
2 tablespoons (15 g) chili powder
1½ teaspoons (7.5 g) salt

Mix cornmeal, baking soda, and salt together. Add buttermilk, eggs, and butter, and stir to blend. Set aside.

Place oil in Dutch oven. Add ground beef, onion, and garlic, and cook until beef is browned. Stir in beans, tomatoes, corn, chili powder, and salt. Bring to a boil. Pour cornmeal mixture over hot beef. Cover and bake at 350°F (177°C) for 40 minutes or until cornmeal pulls away from sides.

OLD-FASHIONED SPAGHETTI

Tomato sauces can be hard on cast iron. While the acid in the tomatoes may be tough on the cast-iron surface, I find that my well-seasoned pot doesn't seem to have a problem with it, especially if I clean it promptly and oil the surface after using. I still cook in the Dutch oven I inherited from my mom, and she cooked this sauce more times than I can remember.

2 pounds (900 g) lean ground beef
1 medium onion, chopped
3 cloves garlic, peeled and crushed
2 (14½ ounce) (820 g) cans diced tomatoes
1 (6-ounce) (170-g) can tomato paste
1 cup (236 g) red wine
1 cup (236 g) beef stock
1 tablespoon (1.6 g) dried basil
1 tablespoon (1.6 g) dried oregano

1 (16-ounce) (453-g) package spaghetti
1 cup (180 g) grated Parmesan

Cook ground beef with onion and garlic until beef is browned. Add tomatoes, tomato paste, wine, stock, basil, and oregano into beef mixture. Simmer 2 hours.

Cook pasta in a second pot of salted water. Drain most of the water from the pot. Ladle spaghetti sauce into pot and toss into pasta. Add cheese and toss again.

CORNED BEEF WITH CABBAGE AND POTATOES

We make a more elaborate version of corned beef in our restaurant, but making your own corned beef doesn't have to be complicated. This simple version of corned beef is perfect for camping. Start the brining process before you leave home. The beef is ready for the pot in just a few days.

Brine:
8 cups (1.9 L) water
1 cup (1.9 kg) kosher salt
⅓ cup (70 g) brown sugar
½ cup (118 mL) white vinegar
¼ cup (25 g) pickling spice

6–8 pounds (2.5–3.5 kg) beef brisket
3 carrots, peeled and cut into 3 in. (7.6 cm) chunks
1 large onion, peeled and quartered
Water
Whole cabbage, cut into large wedges
6 red potatoes, cut in half

Combine water, salt, sugar, vinegar, and pickling spice. Bring to a boil, stirring until sugar and salt are dissolved. Set aside and let cool.

Poke holes in the beef and place into a large resealable plastic bag. Pour in the brine and seal, making sure beef is completely covered and all excess air is removed. Refrigerate for 3–7 days.

When ready to cook, remove beef from bag and rinse off the brine. Place in the Dutch oven and add carrots and onions. Add enough cold water to cover beef. Bring to a boil, then cover and simmer for 2–3 hours. Skim foam off the surface. Add cabbage and potatoes, and cook for another hour or so, until beef and vegetables are tender.

Serve with Horseradish Cream (see page 108).

HORSERADISH CREAM

1 cup (242 g) sour cream
2 tablespoons (30 g) prepared horseradish
Salt and freshly ground black pepper

Mix sour cream and horseradish. Add salt and pepper to taste. Cover and chill up to 2 days. Use with corned beef, on roast beef sandwiches, or to add a zing to mashed potatoes.

COTTAGE PIE

It's called Shepherd's Pie with ground lamb and Good Shepherd's Pie when made with vegetables alone. But my favorite is still the humble beef-based Cottage Pie. I go heavy on the mashed potatoes to satisfy all those end-of-the-day hunger pangs.

3 pounds (1.3 kg) potatoes, peeled and quartered
Water for boiling potatoes
½ cup (118 mL) milk
4 tablespoons (60 g) butter
Salt and black pepper
2 tablespoons (25 g) vegetable oil
1 medium onion, chopped
2 carrots, diced
2 pounds (900 g) ground beef
2 tablespoons (12 g) flour
1 tablespoon (13 g) tomato paste
1½ cups (354 mL) beef stock

1 teaspoon (3 g) freshly chopped thyme leaves
½ cup (75 g) green peas (optional)
½ cup (75 g) corn kernels (optional)
1 cup (120 g) cheddar cheese, shredded

Boil the potatoes until soft. Drain water from pot and mash potatoes, adding milk and butter until they are at the consistency you want. Season with salt and pepper to taste and set aside.

Place vegetable oil in 12 in. (30.5 cm) Dutch oven and sauté onion and carrots until onion starts to soften. Add the ground beef and stir until meat has been browned. Sprinkle the flour onto the meat, stirring to coat. Add the tomato paste, beef stock, thyme, and peas and corn (if using), and season with salt and pepper. Cover and cook over heat for 15 minutes.

Add the mashed potatoes to the top of the meat, using the back of a wooden spoon to cover it completely and form a seal around the edges. Cover and bake at 350°F (177°C) for about 30 minutes. Add shredded cheese to the top and continue to cook, covered, until cheese is melted, about 10 minutes.

LAMB WITH COFFEE AND CURRANT JELLY GLAZE

One day, we left our friend Roger back at camp while we went fishing. When we returned, he surprised us with this dish. The strong perfume of coffee and port, combined with the tangy currant jelly, performed magic on the leg of lamb.

1 (4-pound) (2-kg) leg of lamb
4 cloves garlic
2 tablespoons (15 g) dry mustard
2 tablespoons (15 g) ground ginger
Salt and black pepper
1(10-ounce) (280-g) jar currant jelly
½ cup (118 mL) tawny port
½ cup (118 mL) strong espresso coffee

Place the Dutch oven on the coals to preheat while preparing the leg. Cut slits into lamb and insert garlic cloves. Combine mustard, ginger, salt, and pepper and rub over the surface of the lamb. Place leg into hot oven and cover. Cover and roast about 30 minutes.

While the lamb is roasting, make glaze. Combine jelly, port, and coffee in a small pot and heat through until jelly is melted.

Baste the leg with the sauce every 15 minutes or so, until the leg is cooked to your liking. Medium rare should take just a little over an hour. Check with a meat thermometer—rare is about 140°F (68°C), medium 160°F (78°C). Remove the leg from the oven when it gets close to your desired temperature; even out of the oven, it will continue to cook. Let rest for 10 minutes before carving. Serve with leftover glaze.

SLOW-ROASTED ELK WITH PORT AND APRICOT SAUCE

When we lived in Montana, it was common for us to have elk. I sometimes don't care for wild game, but this recipe produces a tender, flavorful roast that doesn't taste gamey.

1 (4-pound) (2-kg) elk roast
Salt and pepper
2 medium onions, quartered
4 carrots, cut into chunks
4 stalks celery, cut into chunks

Sauce:

2 tablespoons (30 g) butter

½ cup (118 mL) port

1 cup (236 mL) beef stock

1 tablespoon (15 g) tomato paste

4 tablespoons (60 g) apricot jam

1 tablespoon (15 mL) hot sauce

Rub roast with salt and pepper, and place in the Dutch oven. Surround it with vegetables and add water to cover the entire roast. Cover and slow roast at 300°F (148°C)

for 5 hours. When the meat is done, remove it from the oven onto a platter. Discard the vegetables and juices. Let the roast rest for 10 minutes, then slice and serve with sauce.

To make sauce:

Melt butter in Dutch oven and add port and beef stock. Boil to reduce by half. Add tomato paste, apricot jam, and hot sauce, stirring to blend well. Cook until thickened.

VENISON MEATLOAF WITH WILD MUSHROOM GRAVY

This basic meatloaf recipe works with any kind of ground meat. And if wild mushrooms aren't available, just substitute regular white mushrooms.

1½ pounds (725 g) ground venison
1 cup (60 g) bread crumbs
1¼ cups (300 mL) milk
1 egg
1 small onion, diced
1 tablespoon (15 mL) Worcestershire sauce
¾ teaspoon (3.5 g) salt
½ teaspoon (2 g) dry mustard
½ teaspoon (2.5 g) black pepper

Mix all ingredients and form into loaf. Place on rack inside a 10 in. (25.5 cm) Dutch oven. Bake at 350°F (177°C) for 1 hour.

WILD MUSHROOM GRAVY

2 tablespoons (30 mL) vegetable oil

2 cups (150 g) wild mushrooms, coarsely chopped

2 tablespoons flour

1 cup (236 mL) beef stock

Splash of red wine (optional)

Salt and pepper to taste

Pour oil into Dutch oven. Dust mushrooms with flour and sauté in oil until mushrooms are soft and mixture is bubbly. Stir stock and wine into pot, stirring until sauce reaches the correct consistency. Salt and pepper as desired. Serve over meatloaf.

CHAPTER 8

Pork

The flavor of garlic works beautifully with pork and other meat dishes. Unfortunately, its strong, pungent odor often causes people to shy away from using it. I have to admit, there is nothing worse than garlic that has been overcooked in oil. It gets bitter very quickly if browned.

But there is a much better way to enjoy all the goodness of garlic without the strong taste. Roasting whole heads of garlic produces a rich, caramelized flavor that mellows the garlic and removes any hint of bitterness. I roast whole heads of garlic to add to soups and sauces, to whip into mashed potatoes, and to blend into butter. To me, it is the best possible way to add garlic to almost any dish.

Roasted garlic is great served on its own, too. Just squeeze a clove onto a toasted round of bread, and finish with a little salt and pepper for an interesting munch while other courses are cooking.

To make roasted garlic, take a whole head of garlic and peel some of the papery skin off the outside. Cut ½ in. (1.2 cm) off the top of the head, exposing the top of the cloves. Place each head on a square of aluminum foil. Drizzle with olive oil, and season with salt and pepper. Roast heads of garlic, cut side up, right on the grill. Don't place right over direct heat; find a hot location away from flame. (I sometimes put a foil packet inside the Dutch oven with other food.) Roast 45–60 minutes, rotating periodically, until garlic is soft and caramelized. To use, pull out cloves and squeeze out of their skins.

ROASTED PORK WITH APPLES

A delicious way to roast pork—apples and a touch of honey add just a hint of sweetness.

½ cup (118 mL) vegetable oil
4–5 pounds (1.8–2.3 kg) pork roast
Salt and pepper
2 onions, thinly sliced
2 apples, peeled and sliced
2 cups (475 mL) chicken stock
1 tablespoon (15 mL) honey
2 tablespoons (30 mL) soy sauce
2 large carrots, cut into 1 in. (2.5 cm) lengths
4 red potatoes, cut into 1 in. (2.5 cm) chunks

Rub salt and pepper over the pork. Heat the oil and brown roast on all sides to seal in the juices. Remove the roast and set aside. Add onions and apples, and sauté until the onions soften, about 5 minutes. Place the roast back in the oven resting on top of the onions and apples. Combine the chicken stock, honey, and soy sauce, and pour over the roast. Cover and bake at 325°F (163°C) for about 2½ hours. Turn roast and check liquid every 45 minutes or so, adding stock as necessary.

If you wish, add carrots and potatoes to the pot during the last hour of cooking, arranging them around the outside of the roast.

ROSEMARY GARLIC PORK TENDERLOIN

Garlic and rosemary—what a lovely combination. I love the smell of rosemary, so I always carry stems of it to add to the pot when roasting pork. The result is a fragrant, flavorful sauce.

3 tablespoons (45 mL) oil
1 large pork tenderloin (4–5 pounds) (1.8–2.3 kg)
3 tablespoons (45 mL) olive oil
3 tablespoons (7.5 g) chopped rosemary leaves
3 tablespoons (45 g) coarse mustard
6 cloves garlic, minced

½ teaspoon (2.5 g) salt
Black pepper

Place Dutch oven on coals and add oil. Place loin in oven and sear, turning to brown all sides. Combine olive oil, rosemary leaves, mustard, garlic, salt, and black pepper. Rub over top of loin. Roast at 325°F (163°C) for about 2 to 2½ hours, basting occasionally. Remove loin from oven and let rest before slicing. Top with any remaining pan sauce.

CAMP COOT

A campfire variation on the French choucroute garnie—*the perfect pot to put over the fire for a long day at camp.*

1 medium onion, thinly sliced
2 pounds (1 kg) prepared sauerkraut, drained
2 teaspoons (10 g) caraway seeds
1 pound (450 g) red potatoes, scrubbed and cut into
    thick slices
2 pounds (1.2 kg) pork spare-ribs
2 pounds (1 kg) kielbasa, bratwurst, or other sausage,
    cut into 3 in. (7.5 cm) pieces
1 cup (236 mL) chicken broth
1 cup (236 mL) white wine
Salt and black pepper
Grainy mustard

Place the sliced onion in the bottom of the pot. Mix sauerkraut and caraway seeds together. Add the sauerkraut/caraway blend to form the next layer, and do a few grinds of black pepper over the kraut. Next, layer potato slices over the sauerkraut. Salt and pepper the potato layer. Arrange the spare-ribs and sausage over the potatoes in a single layer. Pour the chicken broth and wine on top.

Cover and hang Dutch oven on tripod. Cook over low heat for several hours, until the spare-ribs are fork-tender.

Serve out of the pot, making sure everyone gets some of each of the sausages, ribs, potatoes, and sauerkraut. Pass grainy mustard and crusty bread to complete the meal.

BEER-B-CUE PULLED PORK

This simple pulled pork is the base for a great sandwich. Stack high on a crusty roll with coleslaw and top with your favorite barbecue sauce for a hearty meal.

3 pounds (1.5 kg) pork tenderloin
1 medium onion, sliced into thin rings
1 (12-ounce) (354-mL) bottle beer

Put pork and onion into Dutch oven and pour beer over the top. Bake at 325°F (163°C) for about 2 hours, or until pork can easily be shredded with a fork. Serve on sandwich rolls with a squeeze of barbecue sauce and vinegar-based coleslaw, such as Classic Carolina Slaw (see page 123).

KATE'S BARBECUE SAUCE

This Kansas City–style 'cue sauce is tangy and sweet, with a hint of heat underneath.

4 tablespoons (48 g) oil
1 small onion, finely chopped
2 cloves garlic, peeled and minced
2 cups (480 mL) tomato sauce
½ cup (118 mL) apple juice
½ cup (118 mL) apple cider vinegar
½ cup (100 g) brown sugar
1 teaspoon (5 g) salt
2 tablespoons (12 g) paprika
1 tablespoon (6 g) chili powder
Cayenne pepper

Sauté onion in oil until soft. Add garlic and sauté for another 2 minutes. Add tomato sauce, apple juice, and vinegar. Stir in brown sugar, salt, paprika, and chili powder. Simmer on low heat for 30 minutes or so. Before serving, add cayenne to taste.

CLASSIC CAROLINA SLAW

When it comes to these sandwiches, creamy slaw just won't do.

1 cup (236 mL) apple cider vinegar
1 cup (200 g) sugar
1 teaspoon (5 g) salt

½ cup (118 mL) vegetable oil
1 teaspoon (3 g) dry mustard
1 teaspoon (3 g) celery seed
1 large head of cabbage, finely shredded
1 medium onion, finely chopped

Combine vinegar, sugar, salt, oil, dry mustard, and celery seed in a saucepan and put on low heat. Simmer until sugar is dissolved. Remove from heat and cool completely. Pour cooled vinegar dressing over cabbage and onion in a bowl. Toss and refrigerate until ready to eat.

PORK ROAST WITH APPLES, SAUERKRAUT, AND POTATOES

My dad's German roots gave me this recipe—the hearty combination of tangy kraut and sweet apples makes a warm, comforting fall meal. If I have bratwurst or Polish sausage along, I will tuck hunks of sausage into the pot as well.

3 tablespoons (45 mL) oil
3 pounds (1.3 kg) pork roast
1 pound (450 g) sauerkraut, drained
2 large red apples, sliced
1 medium onion, sliced
½ cup (100 g) brown sugar
1 cup (236 mL) apple cider
3 pounds (1.3 kg) red potatoes

Place oil in hot Dutch oven. Add pork roast, turning to brown on all sides. Mix the sauerkraut, apple, onion, and brown sugar in a bowl. Arrange sauerkraut mixture around roast. Add apple cider and cover. Bake at 350°F (177°C) for 2 hours. Half an hour before serving, add quartered red potatoes around roast. Cover and cook until potatoes are tender.

DUTCH OVEN BARBECUE PORK RIBS

4 pounds (2 kg) meaty pork loin ribs
1 medium onion, quartered
3 carrots, chopped

4 cups (1 L) water

1 (12-ounce) (354-mL) bottle beer

3 cups (700 mL) of your favorite barbecue sauce

Place ribs, onion, carrots, water, and beer into Dutch oven. Cover and bake at 325°F (163°C) for about 1½ hours. When ribs are tender, remove oven from heat and drain excess grease from ribs. Place back on heat and top with barbecue sauce. Cover and cook for another 20 minutes until sauce is nicely thickened.

CHAPTER 9

Chicken

Stacking your Dutch ovens is a fun way to make a multiple-course meal. It also has the advantage of making the most of your coals by making them do double duty. We rarely cook a roast without stacking an oven full of something or other with it.

The coals on the lid of your first oven serve as the bottom coals for the oven stacked on top. Because the top oven helps to trap heat for the oven below, you may not need quite as many coals on the top of the first oven as you would if the oven was by itself. It is a bit of a juggling act, so some experimentation will be needed. Part of the fun is watching over your ovens, moving coals as needed, and rotating them to maintain even heat. Your reward? A whole meal cooked all at once!

Confused yet? Let me give you an example. Put scalloped potatoes in a 14 in. (35.5 cm) Dutch oven with 12 coals below and 12 coals on top. Next place your roast chicken in a 12 in. (30.5 cm) Dutch oven and place it on top of the first oven. The second oven now has 12 coals below. Add 10 coals on top. On top of that, add a 10 in. (25.5 cm) oven, filled with collard greens. Your whole stack can cook together for an hour and a half or so.

Don't start with baked goods in your stack. Baked goods are a little fussier about their heat, so try stacking

with a couple of forgiving recipes first. A nice beef roast goes nicely with an oven of squash or braised onions on top. When I first started stacking, I found that my main problem was often too much heat rather than too little. But roasts and stewed vegetables can have coals pulled or added without much detriment. If all else fails, the whole oven can simply be pulled off if it is cooking too fast!

ROAST CHICKEN WITH ONIONS

This roasted chicken is the perfect beginner's Dutch oven dinner. Just season well and cook slowly for a moist, delectable bird. No need to baste or add liquids—the onions and chicken do all the work. I keep a batch of my poultry rub in the pantry to make chicken preparation quick and easy.

1 large (5–6 pound) (2.5–3.0 kg) roasting chicken
Olive oil
3 tablespoons (18 g) poultry rub (see page 131)
2 large onions, sliced

Prepare the chicken by removing giblets and washing chicken. Pat dry.

Rub olive oil and poultry rub onto the chicken. Place in large plastic resealable bag and refrigerate overnight.

When you are ready to roast the chicken, place the sliced onions into the bottom of the pot. Nestle the chicken into the bed of onions.

Plan on about 20 minutes of cooking time per pound, then add another 10–15 minutes. For a 5-pound (2.5-kg) bird, roasting time should be just under 2 hours. I usually just wiggle the drumstick to test doneness, but if you are uncertain, use a meat thermometer to check the internal temperature. Place a thermometer in the thickest part of the breast. It should read about 160°F (83°C).

When the chicken reaches the proper temperature, remove it, along with most of the onions. Let it rest for 15–20 minutes with a foil tent over it.

While the chicken is resting, make gravy from the drippings.

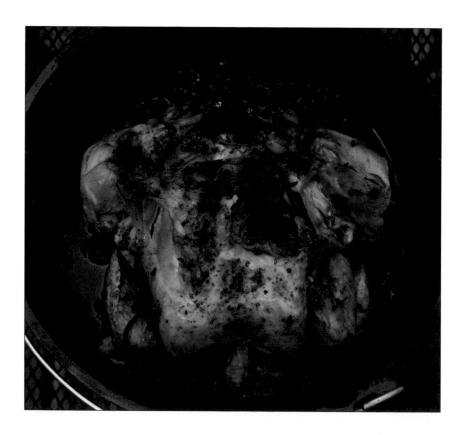

POULTRY RUB BLEND

This recipe makes enough for one roast chicken. If you want to make a batch for your pantry, just triple or quadruple the recipe. Blend all spices and store in an airtight container.

1 teaspoon (3 g) ground sage
2 teaspoons (6 g) paprika
1 teaspoon (3 g) dried thyme
1 tablespoon (15 g) salt
½ teaspoon (2.5 g) black pepper
1 teaspoon (3 g) garlic powder
1 teaspoon (3 g) cayenne pepper

CHICKEN ONION GRAVY

You should have about 1½ cups (354 mL) of juice left in the pan. Remove about ½ cup (118 mL) of juice from the

Dutch oven and whisk in 2–3 tablespoons (12–18 g) flour to create a smooth paste. Blend the paste back into the juice in the pan, and stir until it starts to thicken. Simmer 10 minutes or so until you have reached the desired consistency. Season with salt and pepper and serve.

CHICKEN AND DUMPLINGS

To me, chicken and dumplings are the ultimate comfort food; the perfect pot for chilly evenings on the river.

1 cup (100 g) flour
2 teaspoons (10 g) salt
½ teaspoon (1.5 g) fresh thyme
¼ teaspoon (1.25 g) pepper
4 boneless chicken breasts
Oil
1 cup (236 mL) chicken stock

Dumplings:
1½ cups (150 g) flour
2 teaspoons (8 g) baking powder
½ teaspoon (2.5 g) salt
3 tablespoons (42 g) butter
¾ cup (354 mL) milk

Mix flour, salt, thyme, and pepper. Coat chicken with flour mixture. Heat oil in 12 in. (30.5 cm) Dutch oven. Brown chicken on all sides. Add chicken stock. Cover and simmer over low heat for about an hour.

To make dumplings, mix flour, baking powder, and salt. Cut in butter to make fine crumbs. Stir in milk to make soft dough. Drop dumpling mixture into the pot in large spoonfuls, distributing them evenly over the top of the simmering chicken. Cover the pot and simmer for 10 minutes, then uncover and simmer 10 more minutes. Dumplings will swell to fill the top of the pot.

CHICKEN WITH 40 CLOVES OF GARLIC

Does garlic really repel mosquitoes? That was our theory the first time we tried this classic French recipe at camp. As it turns out, it doesn't really matter—this dish is so good, we'll eat it any time, even without mosquitoes around.

4 pounds (2 kg) chicken breasts, bone-in
Salt and pepper
2 tablespoons (30 mL) olive oil
40 peeled cloves garlic
2 fresh parsley sprigs
1 fresh rosemary sprig
1 fresh thyme sprig
1 fresh sage sprig
1 cup (236 mL) dry white wine
1 loaf crusty bread or baguette

Season chicken pieces with salt and pepper. Toss with olive oil and brown on both sides in Dutch oven over high heat. Tie the fresh herbs together into a bouquet and add to the pot, along with the garlic cloves. Top with

white wine. Cover and bake at 325°F (163°C) for about 1½ hours. Serve chicken with pan juices and spread garlic cloves onto rounds of fresh crusty bread.

CHICKEN POT PIE

You can use refrigerated crescent rolls or even phyllo dough for your top crust, but I prefer a traditional crust—rolled a little thick and brushed with butter.

2 tablespoons (30 mL) vegetable oil

1 medium onion, chopped

1 pound (450 g) boneless, skinless chicken breast cut in 1 in. (2.5 cm) pieces

3 medium potatoes, 1 in. (2.5 cm) dice

2 carrots, sliced

1½ cups (354 mL) chicken broth

½ teaspoon (1.5 g) dried thyme

2 tablespoons (18 g) cornstarch

1 cup (475 mL) milk

½ cup (50 g) frozen peas

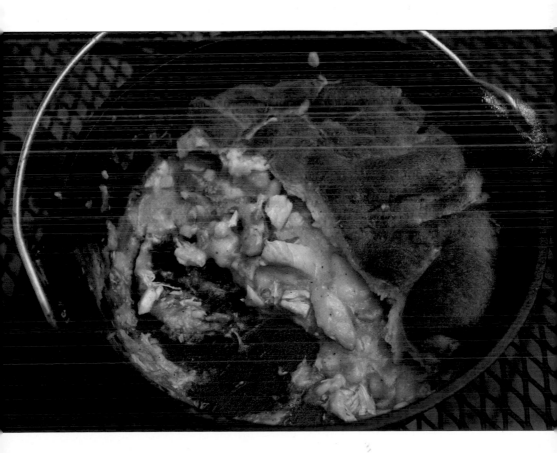

½ cup (50 g) frozen corn
Salt and pepper
1 pie crust, or other dough for topping

Heat the oil in a large saucepan over medium-high heat. Add the onion and sauté until soft. Add the chicken breast and cook until the chicken is seared on all sides. Add potatoes, carrots, chicken broth, and thyme. Cover and simmer until the vegetables are tender.

Remove 1 cup of juice from pan and whisk in cornstarch. Stir back into the pot. Add milk and stir until nicely thickened. Stir in the peas and corn, and heat through. Season to taste with salt and pepper.

Roll out crust to fit and place over the stew. Cover and bake at 350°F (177°C) for 30–40 minutes or until crust is nicely browned.

CHICKEN AND RICE CASSEROLE

Quick and easy one-pot goodness.

1 (10½-ounce) (300-mL) can cream of mushroom soup
½ cup (125 g) sour cream
2 cups (475 mL) chicken broth
1 cup (210 g) uncooked rice
4 split chicken breasts, bone-in
2 tablespoons (30 mL) melted butter
Poultry seasoning

Mix cream of mushroom soup, sour cream, chicken broth, and rice. Pour into 10 in. (25.5 cm) Dutch oven. Arrange chicken pieces on top. Brush chicken with melted butter and sprinkle with poultry seasoning. Bake at 350°F (177°C) for about an hour, or until rice is firm but tender and chicken is cooked through.

CHAPTER 10

Seafood

Most of our fish dishes are the quick-cooking type. Cast-iron skillets are ideal for searing fresh fish. A handful of shrimp is transformed in a hot pan in just a few minutes. And of course, the Dutch oven is the ideal tool for frying a big batch of fish.

New England has its clambakes. Louisiana has its crawfish boils. Wisconsin is known for its fish fries. In fact, it is almost impossible to go out on Friday night and choose something other than fish. A traditional fish fry includes french fries, coleslaw, hush puppies, lemon wedges, tartar sauce, and malt vinegar.

Of course, the best way to have a fish fry is when the fish is fresh out of the water. We fried smelt on the shores of Lake Superior on my prom night. We cooked luxurious steaks of tender white walleye every opening weekend on Lake of the Woods. And our summers were devoted to the delicate curls of sunfish fillets, caught by the boatful on Spooner Lake and served with hush puppies and plenty of cold beer.

There is nothing better for deep frying than a cast iron Dutch oven. Choose your largest diameter oven to give your fish plenty of room. Add fresh oil, filling the oven almost halfway. Heat the oil so that a splash of water sputters energetically. Drop battered fish pieces in one at a time, making sure not to crowd the pieces. You want your oil to bubble up around each piece. Flip the fillets with tongs to brown both sides, and use a big mesh skimmer to remove fish from the oil and place on paper towels to drain.

WISCONSIN FISH FRY

If it is Friday night in Wisconsin, it must be fish. Our Friday night fish fries were legendary events. I am not sure where we got this recipe using 7 Up, but we've been using it forever. It creates a light crisp crust with a little bit of sweetness that I love. It's great with shrimp, too. If you prefer, replace the 7 Up with beer.

1–2 pounds (450–900 g) white fish fillets
Pancake mix in plastic bag for coating
1 egg
1 cup (130 g) pancake mix
1 cup (236 mL) 7 Up
Oil, for frying

Dredge fish fillets in dry pancake mix and set aside. Blend egg, pancake mix, and 7 Up.

Dip fillets into batter and place gently into hot oil. Fry for about 5 minutes, turning once. Remove from oil and place on paper towels to drain. Serve with tartar sauce or malt vinegar.

ROASTED MUSSELS WITH LEMON-GARLIC BUTTER

If you are accustomed to steaming your mussels, try this method instead. Pan-roasting them over high heat concentrates their flavor and enhances the buttery sauce.

½ cup (115 g) butter, softened
2 shallots, finely chopped
4 cloves garlic, minced
¼ cup (20 g) fresh parsley, minced
2 tablespoons (6 g) chives, minced
1 teaspoon (2 g) dried thyme leaves
1 tablespoon (10 g) lemon rind, grated
2 tablespoons (30 mL) lemon juice
4 pounds (2 kg) mussels

In a bowl, cream together butter, shallots, garlic, parsley, chives, thyme, lemon rind, and lemon juice. Set aside.

Heat 12 in. (30.5 cm) Dutch oven on coals until very hot. Place cleaned mussels in oven and cover, cooking until they open—about 10 minutes. Toss the butter

mixture into the mussels, stirring to coat. Discard any mussels that don't open.

Serve with crunchy bread for dipping into juices.

HADDOCK WITH CREAM

Even our non-fish eaters like this recipe. So good—serve with a squeeze of lemon, a side of rice pilaf, and sautéed spinach.

2 pounds (1 kg) haddock fillets
1 tablespoon (3 g) parsley, chopped
3 tablespoons (45 g) finely chopped shallots
Salt and pepper
½ cup (130 mL) heavy cream
2 tablespoons (30 g) butter
Bread crumbs (optional)

Line a 10 in. (25.5 cm) Dutch oven with parchment paper. Place the fish in the bottom of the oven and add parsley, shallots, salt, and pepper. Pour the cream over the fish and add little pats of butter. Cover and bake for about 30 minutes. If you wish, add bread crumbs to the top and finish by browning the topping with a kitchen blowtorch.

SEAFOOD STEW

We like to make this with whatever we've caught or collected that day—a great stew for camping oceanside. We have even made it with conch and jack fish caught off the Bahamian coast.

¼ cup (60 mL) olive oil

1 cup (150 g) celery, chopped

1 green pepper, chopped

2 medium onions, chopped

2 cloves garlic, minced

1 (28-ounce) (790-g) can plum tomatoes

1 cup (236 mL) chicken broth

1 cup (236 mL) white wine

1 bay leaf

1 teaspoon (3 g) basil

1 dozen cherrystone clams or mussels

½ pound (225 g) kielbasa, cut into 1 in. (2.5 cm) chunks

1 pound (450 g) shrimp, shelled

1 pound (450 g) white fish, cut into 2 in. (5.0 cm) squares

Sauté celery, pepper, onions, and garlic in oil until vegetables start to soften. Add tomatoes, chicken broth, wine, bay leaf, and basil. Cover and simmer 30 minutes. Add clams and chunks of kielbasa, covering until the clams open, about 5 minutes. Add shrimp and chunks of fish and cook for another 10 minutes or so. Serve over rice.

JAMBALAYA

Cajun recipes like this one all start with a Cajun mirepoix—*onions, green bell pepper, and celery. (I personally prefer the gentle flavor of red bell pepper). My mother's recipe called for three kinds of meat plus shrimp. But this recipe can be adapted any way you like. Just make sure to include at least one nice smoky choice.*

1 tablespoon (15 mL) olive oil

1 large onion, diced

1 green or red bell pepper, diced

2 stalks celery, diced

2 cloves garlic, minced

½ pound (225 g) ham, diced

½ pound (225 g) kielbasa or andouille sausage

1 pound (450 g) boneless chicken breast, cut into small chunks

1 cup (160 g) diced tomatoes

½ cup (118 mL) tomato sauce

2½ cups (600 mL) chicken broth

2 tablespoons (6 g) Cajun seasoning

1 cup (145 g) uncooked long-grain converted rice
1 pound (450 g) peeled and deveined medium shrimp

Sauté the onion, pepper, celery, and garlic until soft. Add ham, sausage, and chicken, and cook until chicken is seared on all sides. Add tomatoes, tomato sauce, and chicken broth, and season with Cajun seasoning. Bring to a boil and stir in the rice. Cover, reduce heat, and simmer for about 30 minutes. Rice should be tender but not mushy, and most of the liquid should be absorbed. Add the shrimp and cook, covered, until shrimp is cooked through.

CHAPTER 11

Dessert

They say that cooking is an art, but baking is a science. I love to bake in the Dutch oven, but I will admit that baked goods have been my biggest source of cooking failure! Unlike roasts and stews, which will tolerate changes in heat and movement, the average cake can be fairly demanding. Constant, steady heat is called for when baking. It is all too easy to find that you have burned the bottom, or that the top is still not quite done. I tend to use dessert recipes that call for fruit, as well as those that benefit from moist heat, like bread pudding. The Dutch oven seems to be made for them. Make sure to preheat your oven and take special care to get the lid hot. Charcoal proportions are very important. You will use 3–4 briquettes on top of the oven to every 1 briquette you use on the bottom.

Some people place cake pans right inside their oven, but I always use parchment paper to line the oven. Parchment allows you to quickly remove the cake from the hot oven. There are no pans to clean and the parchment peels easily off the cake.

Celebrating special events outdoors is such a treat. We travel with a small culinary blowtorch in our pantry kit. The blowtorch allows us to crust up toppings that might not brown to our liking inside the oven. With it, a sprinkle

of sugar or a crumble topping can be quickly broiled to a pleasing brown.

To create an extravagant birthday cake, finish with flaming liquor. To do this, pour ½ cup (118 mL) of brandy into a small pan away from any open flame, then place on low heat to warm. Light the brandy inside the pan and pour over the warm cake.

WILD BLUEBERRY DUMPLINGS

When the blueberries are ripe, they go from berry bush to Dutch oven in record time. We have many favorite recipes, but these simple dumplings are a favorite.

4 cups (400 g) fresh blueberries
1 cup (200 g) sugar
¼ teaspoon (1.25 g) salt
½ teaspoon (3 g) lemon zest
2 cups (200 g) flour
4 teaspoons (45 g) baking powder
¼ teaspoon (1 g) cinnamon
2 tablespoons (24 g) sugar
1 teaspoon (5 g) salt
4 tablespoons (60 g) butter, softened
1 cup (236 mL) milk
1 tablespoon (12 g) sugar

In a 10 in. (25.5 cm) Dutch oven, combine the blueberries, sugar, salt, and lemon zest. Stir and simmer until the sugar is dissolved and starts to form a syrup. In a bowl, combine flour, baking powder, cinnamon, sugar, and salt. Cut in the butter so that the dough forms a fine crumble. Add the milk and stir just until mixed. Drop dough by spoonfuls into the hot blueberry mixture, and sprinkle with sugar. Cover immediately so the dumplings can start to steam. They will puff up to delicate, soft crowns. Bake at 350°F (177°C) for 30 minutes. Serve with a dollop of whipped cream.

PINEAPPLE UPSIDE-DOWN CAKE

An old-fashioned classic, perfect for Dutch oven–style cooking.

¼ cup (60 g) butter, melted

½ cup (100 g) brown sugar

1 (6-ounce) (170-g) can pineapple rings

½ cup (60 g) pecans

1¼ cups (130 g) flour

¾ cup (150 g) sugar

2 teaspoons (8 g) baking powder

¼ teaspoon (1.25 g) salt

1 egg

1 teaspoon (5 mL) vanilla

½ cup (118 mL) milk

1 tablespoon (15 g) butter

Line 12 in. (30.5 cm) Dutch oven with parchment liner. Add butter and brown sugar to bottom of oven. Arrange the pineapple rings in the bottom of the pot, and sprinkle on pecans. Beat together remaining ingredients to make cake batter. Pour batter over pineapple. Bake at 350°F (177°C) for 25–30 minutes. To serve, lift cake out of the oven and flip over onto a plate. Remove parchment and serve.

APPLE-GINGERBREAD UPSIDE-DOWN CAKE

Gingerbread is one of my favorite desserts, made all the better with a layer of caramel-y apples on top. To make it extra-special, top with whipped cream.

½ cup (100 g) sugar

½ cup (130 g) butter, softened

1 egg

1 cup (236 mL) molasses

2½ cups (250 g) flour

1½ teaspoons (6 g) baking soda

½ teaspoon (2.5 g) salt

1 teaspoon (3 g) cinnamon

1 teaspoon (3 g) ginger

½ teaspoon (2 g) ground cloves

1 cup (236 mL) hot water

¼ cup (60 g) butter

½ cup (100 g) brown sugar

4 cups (720 g) peeled and chopped apples

Make cake batter: In a bowl, cream together sugar and butter with a whisk. Beat in egg and molasses. Add flour, baking soda, salt, cinnamon, ginger, and cloves and blend. Stir in the hot water.

Line 12 in. (30.5 cm) Dutch oven with parchment liner. Add butter and brown sugar, stirring to melt butter and coat bottom. Arrange the apples in the bottom of the pot. Pour prepared gingerbread batter on top. Bake at 350°F (177°C) for 1 hour or until toothpick inserted into the center comes out clean. To serve, lift cake out of oven and flip onto plate. Remove parchment and serve with whipped cream.

BREAD PUDDING

This soft, custard-style pudding has rum-soaked raisins and nuts. I always use the Dutch oven to make this recipe, even in my home oven, because the Dutch oven adds steam and creates a moist, delicate dish.

8 cups (475 g) day-old French bread, cut into 2 in.
    (5 cm) chunks

¾ cup (115 g) raisins, soaked for 10 minutes in rum

1 cup (120 g) chopped pecans

5 eggs

¾ cup (150 g) sugar

2½ cups (600 mL) milk

2½ cups (600 mL) heavy cream

1 tablespoon (15 mL) vanilla

¾ teaspoon (3 g) nutmeg

¼ teaspoon (1.25 g) salt

Line 12 in. (30.5 cm) Dutch oven with parchment liner. Toss bread, raisins, and nuts together and place in Dutch oven. Beat eggs and sugar together. Blend in milk and cream and add vanilla, nutmeg, and salt. Pour over bread. Bake at 350°F (177°C) for 45 minutes or until edges are done and center still shakes a little. Remove from oven and serve with whipped cream.

OZARK PUDDING

Not so much pudding as it is part cake, part pecan pie. This recipe came right out of my mother's recipe book. I honestly don't know anything about the Ozark reference, but there is no question the taste is quintessentially Southern.

1½ cups (300 g) sugar

¼ cup (50 g) all-purpose flour

2½ teaspoons (10 g) baking powder

¼ teaspoon (1.25 g) salt

2 eggs

1 teaspoon (15 mL) vanilla

1 medium apple, peeled and chopped

1 cup (120 g) pecans, chopped

Beat sugar, flour, baking powder, salt, eggs, and vanilla together until smooth. Stir in apple and pecans. Pour batter into parchment-lined 10 in. (25.5 cm) Dutch oven. Bake at 350°F (177°C) until top is browned, about 40 minutes. Lift parchment with cake from oven immediately after cooking. Let cool a bit, but serve warm, preferably with whipped cream.

SWEET POTATO PUDDING

On a spooky Halloween night, we lit a path through the forest with glowing jack-o'-lanterns that led to a cozy campsite. We served this dessert—a nod to traditional pumpkin pie.

4½ cups (900 g) raw sweet potatoes, grated
1⅔ cups (400 mL) milk
⅔ cup (160 mL) dark corn syrup
4 eggs
2 tablespoons (30 g) butter
⅔ cup (130 g) brown sugar
1½ teaspoons (6 g) cinnamon
½ teaspoon (2 g) nutmeg
½ teaspoon (2.5 g) salt

Line a 10 in. (25.5 cm) Dutch oven with parchment paper. Mix all ingredients and pour into oven. Bake at 350°F (177°C) for about an hour. Knife inserted into center should come out clean.

BRANDIED CHERRY BAKED APPLES

Beautiful, bright apples baked with dried cherries, pecans, and a splash of brandy—the perfect end to a fall meal.

4 apples (Crispin, Cortland, Gala, or Granny Smith)
½ cup (75 g) dried cherries marinated in brandy overnight
2 tablespoons (15 g) coarsely chopped pecans
3 tablespoons (38 g) brown sugar
Pinch of salt and pepper
1 teaspoon (3 g) nutmeg
4 tablespoons (60 g) unsalted butter
⅔ cup (160 mL) apple cider

Core the apples, making sure not to cut through the bottoms. Peel them down to the halfway mark. In a small bowl, mix together the cherries, pecans, brown sugar, salt, pepper, nutmeg, and butter. Divide the mixture among the apples. Arrange the apples in the Dutch oven and pour in the cider. Bake at 350°F (177°C) for about an hour, or until apples are tender. Remove apples from oven. Boil the juices for a few minutes to make a more concentrated sauce. Pour sauce over the apples and serve.

PLUM TART

This simple tart is a lovely way to enhance the taste of fresh plums. Even better if you can use wild plums. They are a little smaller, though, so increase to 6 or 8 plums.

3 plums cut into wedges
⅔ cup (150 g) light brown sugar
2 tablespoons (8 g) cornstarch
¼ teaspoon (1 g) cinnamon
¼ teaspoon (1 mL) lemon juice
1⅓ cups (130 g) all-purpose flour
½ cup (100 g) granulated sugar
½ teaspoon (2.5 g) salt
½ cup (120 g) cold unsalted butter, cubed
¼ cup (60 mL) ice water, or as needed
Milk and sugar, to glaze crust

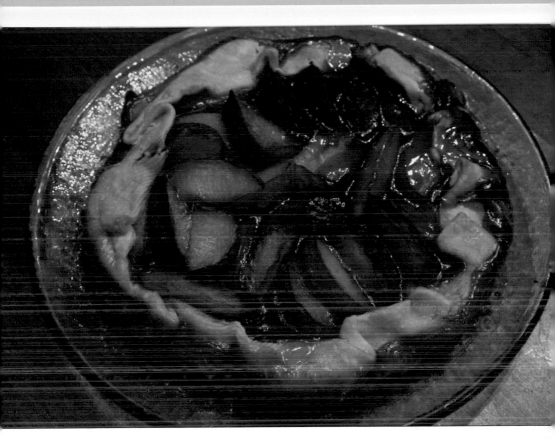

Preheat Dutch oven and lid. In a bowl, combine plums, brown sugar, cornstarch, cinnamon, and lemon juice until evenly coated. Set aside.

Stir together the flour, sugar, and salt with a fork to blend. Cut the butter into the flour using two knives. Add a few tablespoons of the ice water to the flour mixture, and mix gently. Continue to add the water, a tablespoon or so at a time, just until it holds together. Be careful not to overmix. The dough should be evenly moist, not wet, and should appear shaggy or rough in appearance.

Roll out the dough onto the parchment paper into an even circle about 13 in. (33 cm) in diameter and fit into the bottom of the Dutch oven. Place fruit mixture in center, leaving a 1½ in. (2.5–5.0 cm) border around edges. Fold edges of crust over filling, pressing gently to hold the shape. Brush crust edges with milk and sprinkle with sugar. Bake at 350°F (177°C) for 30 minutes.

DARK CHOCOLATE BROWNIES

Who can resist moist, chewy brownies? Make sure to remove them from your Dutch oven as soon as they are done—part of their perfection is keeping them moist and a tiny bit undercooked.

1¼ (250 g) cups sugar
¾ cup (80 g) unsweetened cocoa powder
¼ teaspoon (1.25 g) salt
10 tablespoons (140 g) unsalted butter, melted
½ teaspoon (3 mL) vanilla
2 eggs
½ cup (50 g) flour
½ cup (90 g) dark chocolate chips
½ cup (90 g) white chocolate chips

Combine the sugar, cocoa, and salt in a medium bowl. Add melted butter and mix until smooth. Stir in vanilla. Add the eggs one at a time, stirring vigorously after each one. Blend in flour. Stir in the chocolate chips

Line 10 in. (25.5 cm) Dutch oven with parchment paper. Spread batter evenly in the lined pan. Bake at

350°F (177°C) until a toothpick in the center emerges slightly moist with batter, about 20–25 minutes.

Lift brownies out of the Dutch oven immediately and transfer to a cutting board to cool.

MIXED BERRY CRISP

Any fruit can be substituted in this recipe. Mix and match your berries, or use peaches, apples, or pears. Larger fruits will need to bake a bit longer.

½ cup (120 g) unsalted butter
½ cup (50 g) flour
¾ cup (150 g) brown sugar
1½ cups (120 g) rolled oats
½ teaspoon (2.5 g) salt

¼ teaspoon (1.25 g) fresh ground pepper

1 teaspoon (3 g) ginger

¼ teaspoon (1 g) allspice

¼ cup (60 mL) water

4 teaspoons (16 g) cornstarch

½ cup (100 g) sugar

1 quart (460 g) blueberries

1 quart (460 g) raspberries

1 quart (460 g) blackberries

1 teaspoon (5 mL) vanilla

½ teaspoon (2.5 mL) lemon juice

Cut butter into small pieces. Blend flour, brown sugar, oats, salt, pepper, ginger, and allspice in a bowl. Mix until it looks like coarse meal. Pour in water and mix lightly, then set aside.

Mix cornstarch and sugar in medium bowl. Add berries gently into the cornstarch mix so as not to break berries. Add vanilla and lemon juice.

Pour berry mix into 10 in. (25.5 cm) Dutch oven. Sprinkle the crumb topping over the berries. Cover and bake at 350°F (177°C) for 35 minutes.

GIANT CHEWY CHOCOLATE COOKIE

Cookies in the Dutch oven? Of course—if it's a really big one. Just bake and cut into wedges.

1⅓ cups (130 g) all-purpose flour

¼ teaspoon (1 g) baking soda

¼ teaspoon (1.25 g) salt

¼ cup (60 g) unsalted butter, melted

¼ cup (70 g) packed brown sugar

4 tablespoons (12 g) white sugar

1 teaspoon (5 mL) vanilla

1 egg

1 egg yolk

1 cup (180 g) semisweet chocolate chips

Line 10 in. (25.5 cm) Dutch oven with parchment paper. Mix together the flour, baking soda, and salt. Cream together the melted butter, brown sugar, and white sugar. Beat in the vanilla, egg, and egg yolk until light and creamy. Mix in the dry ingredients until just blended.

Stir in the chocolate chips. Spread cookie mix in the center of the parchment paper, leaving about 1 in. of space around the inside of the Dutch oven. Bake at 350°F (177°C) for 15–20 minutes or until the edges are lightly toasted. Remove immediately and cool for a few minutes before cutting.

Index of Recipes